Burned at the Stake

Burned at the Stake

The Life and Death of Mary Channing

Summer Strevens

PEN & SWORD
HISTORY

First published in Great Britain in 2017 by
Pen & Sword History
An imprint of
Pen & Sword Books Ltd
47 Church Street
Barnsley
South Yorkshire
S70 2AS

Copyright © Summer Strevens, 2017

ISBN 978 1 47389 872 1

A CIP catalogue record for this book is
available from the British Library.

Printed and bound in England
by CPI Group (UK) Ltd, Croydon, CR0 4YY

Pen & Sword Books Ltd incorporates the Imprints of Pen & Sword Books
Archaeology, Atlas, Aviation, Battleground, Discovery, Family History, History,
Maritime, Military, Naval, Politics, Railways, Select, Transport, True Crime,
Fiction, Frontline Books, Leo Cooper, Praetorian Press, Seaforth Publishing,
Wharncliffe and White Owl.

For a complete list of Pen & Sword titles please contact
PEN & SWORD BOOKS LIMITED
47 Church Street, Barnsley, South Yorkshire, S70 2AS, England
E-mail: enquiries@pen-and-sword.co.uk
Website: www.pen-and-sword.co.uk

Contents

Acknowledgements

I must open these acknowledgements with my indebtedness to one who is nameless – the author of the five letters making up the only contemporary publication devoted to the life, trial and execution of Mary Channing, the *Serious Admonitions to Youth*, published in the year of her death. Though their identity is a question yet to be answered, I have tentatively named him in last chapter of this book, the identification made with the assistance of Mike Russell, On-line Parish Clerk for Dorchester & Fordington, to whom I also owe untold thanks for his kindness in allowing me access to his tireless and meticulous research into the life and death of Mary Channing, and for his views, comments and forgiving patience in the face of my many questions, all contributing immeasurably to the writing of this book.

I would also like to express my gratitude to Mr Jim Smith, a descendant of Thomas Brookes, the youngest brother of Mary Channing, for sharing with me the fascinating ancestral links his research has uncovered; the graves of Thomas, his wife Martha and their son Edward can be found in the churchyard of St Michael's at Stinsford near Dorchester, where Thomas Hardy's heart is also interred, alongside the grave of his first wife Emma Lavinia Gifford, and next to whom his second wife, Florence Dugdale Hardy is also buried.

As Hardy's inspirations and writing have been integral to my research (and indeed have provided the title for this book) I must also thank Dr Tony Fincham, Chairman of the Thomas Hardy Society, who has been exploring Hardy's Wessex for the last thirty-five years, and needless to say is an authority on the great man, and proved most obliging in sharing from his own published studies.

I would also like to extend my thanks to Charlotte Green from the Dorset History Centre for her assistance with my enquires into the County archives, as well as Anna Butler, Secretary of the Dorset County Museum, Brian Hellin, Churchwarden at St Peter's, Dorchester and June Jenkins who runs the Parish Office for Dorchester & The Winterbournes Team Ministry.

Thanks are also due to my publishers for their support and encouragement and in particular to my editor Carol Trow for honing the present manuscript.

Finally, I am indebted to my partner, Jack Gritton, without whose help and support, in the face of my woeful IT abilities, I would have been thrown into a familiar panic!

To all those mentioned above, and everyone else who has given of their time, guided and shared in their knowledge and insights, and without whose generosity and goodwill this book might never have been written, Thank You.

Summer Strevens

Introduction

I first came across Mary Channing while researching another book, which, among the other real life inspirations behind some of the characters portrayed in historic and contemporary popular fiction, included the real life inspiration for Thomas Hardy's *Tess of the D'Urbervilles*. Certainly the execution of Martha Brown, the last woman to be publicly hanged in Dorset and witnessed by the fascinated 16-year-old Hardy, amongst an estimated crowd of 4,000 onlookers, made such an impression on the then architecture apprentice that, even seven decades later, Hardy could vividly recall the macabre scene, '...what a fine figure she showed against the sky as she hung in the misty rain and how the tight black silk gown set off her shape as she wheeled half round and back.' Yet the tragic end to Martha Brown's life on that drizzly August morning in 1856, on the gallows erected over the gateway of the new entrance leading to Dorset County Gaol, facilitating the assembled crowds the best possible view, was not the only dark inspiration Hardy drew from the town that he would later immortalise as 'Casterbridge'; details of Mary Channing's execution, the last woman to be strangled and burned at the stake in Dorset not only appearing in *The Mayor of Casterbridge*. Her story was also the inspiration for Hardy's poem *The Mock Wife*.

The heavily attended public burning of the unfortunate 19-year-old Mary Channing took place in 1706, following her conviction for the murder of her husband, she having allegedly poisoned Thomas Channing a little over thirteen weeks after the unsatisfactory marriage into which she had been cajoled by her parents, and at whose feet the blame for the development of Mary's wayward character has also been laid. When brought before the justices, she had the opportunity to defend herself and, according to the presiding judge, apparently did so very capably. She stood little chance against the two barristers and many prosecution witnesses, whose testimony was decidedly coloured by the widely acknowledged tarnish to Mary's character; the jury took only half an hour to find her guilty. Yet on pronouncement of the death sentence, Mary 'pleaded her belly' which meant the postponement of her execution until after she had given birth to her child in gaol, the recourse of many condemned women, understandably desperate to delay the inevitable.

After the birth of her son, whose name was intentionally omitted from the contemporary records in order to provide him with a degree of anonymity in view of his blackened parentage, though Mary was seriously debilitated after the rigours of a prison delivery – childbirth was a risky enough business without the added complications of the prevalent conditions of filth which existed in prisons at the time – her sentence was nevertheless reinstated, and the execution of this weakened and emaciated young woman was made into something of a county fair. The perversely enjoyable distraction of a public execution was a tasteless yet grim reality, one which attracted 10,000 spectators who gathered to view Mary's barbaric ordeal upon the floor of Dorchester's ancient Roman Amphitheatre, Maumbury Rings. Doubtless, the notoriety of the condemned prisoner accounted for the large draw; the ample spectator capacity and the arrangement of this former gladiatorial venue certainly afforded a good view, though the baying masses assembled that afternoon were to be kept waiting for the main event (two prior hangings had taken place at noon) as, incredible as it may seem, Mary's execution was delayed until 5 o'clock while the under-sheriff finished his tea.

In accordance with the death penalty handed down to those found guilty on a count of 'petty treason' and conferred on wives convicted of the murder of their husbands, while the law allowed that Mary be strangled to death by the noose *before* the faggots which had been piled up around her were lit, there is evidence to suggest that she was in fact still alive when consigned to the flames. Yet, in spite of the assumed 'appetite' of the assembled crowd for such a gory spectacle, to quote from Hardy's *Mayor of Casterbridge*, 'not one of those ten thousand people ever cared particularly for hot roast after that'.

Reflecting Hardy's interest in local history and folklore, while the fate of Mary Channing was the basis for *The Mock Wife*, the ballad is in fact constructed around the legend that tells the story of what was supposedly done to satisfy the dying wish of the husband whom Mary had supposedly poisoned, the crux of the poem being that Channing died happy in the belief that his wife, of whom he harboured no suspicion, had kissed him before his death. While Mary's end is only touched upon in the poem, Hardy seems to have been held by an enduring and some would say, grim, fascination with Mary's story, recording some of the grislier details of his research about Mary's execution in his personal notebooks. There were those however who had doubts as to Mary's guilt and it would appear that Hardy was of their number. He was not convinced that she had been given a fair and impartial trial, tainted by the detrimental aspersions universally cast upon her character, nor that the evidence brought against her was anything more than circumstantial, an uncertainty expressed in the final stanza of *The Mock Wife*, the thoughts of some of the anonymous witnesses to her execution obviously reflecting Hardy's own feelings.

The sentencing and execution of Mary Channing also brings into focus the prevalent societal impact of the subordination of women in the eighteenth century; specifically, the prejudicial view taken of female felons by the judiciary, where even modes of execution personified the inequality of the sexes and starkly demonstrated by the death penalty reserved for females found guilty of 'petty treason'. Any woman who killed her husband was thought to have broken the 'natural hierarchy', effectively striking at the very principles of the then perceived social order; as such, a wife was not only guilty of murder but also of 'petty treason' which carried the more severe penalty at the stake. While the capital punishment for husbands found guilty of murdering their wives was hanging from the gallows, until a parliamentary abolition was passed in June 1790, those found guilty of mariticide were still executed by strangulation and their bodies then burned at the stake. However, while the law did extend the clemency of strangulation before the fires were lit, the horrific 'live' burning of Mary Channing was not an isolated case, giving rise to some of the more horrifying accounts that will be related in a later chapter.

The poignancy of *The Mock Wife* notwithstanding, in spite of the enduring fascination with the circumstances of her life and the disturbing details of her death, still capturing the popular imagination, the only written account dedicated solely to Mary Channing was that published in the year of her execution, a 52-page booklet compiled from five letters written at the publisher's behest, the few, though slightly differing, brief accounts appearing in print afterwards all stemming from this 1706 publication.

Certainly, the volubly titled *Serious Admonitions to Youth, In a short Account of the Life, Trial, Condemnation and Execution. Of Mrs. Mary Channing. Who, For Poisoning her Husband, was Burnt at Dorchester in the County of Dorset On thursday, March the 21st 1706 With Practical Reflections* was in much the same vein as those sanctimonious yet sensationalised accounts appearing in various compendiums such as the hugely popular *Newgate Calendar*. Supposedly a moralising publication, nevertheless the *Calendar* gave salacious and vivid accounts of the exploits of infamous criminals in the eighteenth and nineteenth centuries; it was remarked that if an individual owned only two books, while naturally one would be the Bible, the other was the *Newgate Calendar*. Featuring details of historic transgressions as well as the particulars

of contemporary criminals, the introduction to the 1780 edition of the
Newgate *Calendar* ran:

> 'In an age abandoned to dissipation, and when the ties of religion
> and morality fail to have their accustomed influence on the mind,
> the publication of a New Work of his nature makes its appearance
> with peculiar propriety'.

The contents were nonetheless greedily devoured by a public hungry for the
gruesome and gory facts and rumours surrounding high-profile criminals
and their executions. While such publications allowed for vicarious mass
consumption by a widespread readership, they were no substitute for the
real life spectacle and the appetite for public execution was voracious, as
demonstrated by the strength of the crowd on the day that Mary Channing
burned.

While more than 300 years have passed since the disturbing end to her
life, Mary's fate still holds a macabre fascination, as it did for Hardy. The
literary struggles of his imagined tragic characters are more than suggestive of Hardy's responsive sensibilities of those real-life fates befall-
ing such unfortunates as Mary Channing and Martha Brown; this is why
the penultimate chapter of this book is devoted to Hardy's 'Dorchester
Inspirations'. The conjecture surrounding Mary's condemnation (and
indeed that of Martha) still matters today, and the impetus and influences
driving the verdict passed on her are necessarily worthy of examination;
Hardy certainly regarded the case against her as 'not proven', given the
evidence on which she was convicted, Hardy's presumption grounded on
his own judicial experience; in 1883 he accepted a nomination to sit on the
bench as a Justice of the Peace and sat in court at least thirty eight times
as a magistrate. Yet the impaired status of women in eighteenth century
English society was doubtless another overweening factor influencing the
outcome of her case.

Judicial rights or wrongs aside, I also hope to get closer to Mary Channing
herself. While much has been written about Martha Brown, about the
woman herself and her fate as inspiration to Hardy, Mary Channing has
received scant literary attention, though to a degree supposition has necessarily played a large part, given the restrictions of a lack of unbiased contemporary source material. And in researching the life of one who been so
thoroughly denigrated over the years and subject to a damning consensus of
opinion from the very first, maintaining a personal impartiality about her is

something which cannot be lost sight of. While it is necessary on one hand to retain a firm grip on the source material, the distorting pious attitude which was the hallmark of the contemporary literary treatments of lives such as Mary's can be an impediment. This is why it is essential that we try to build a coherent picture of a person's life and character based on their actions, priorities, decisions, and their defiance of (or compliance with) contemporary mores, serving to give us an insight into a personal history, which in Mary's case I hope this book has gone some way towards achieving. Indeed, if the colourful accounts of her life are to be believed, she was certainly of a recalcitrant inclination, what we might term today as a 'tearaway teenager' or 'wild child', and she certainly provided much for the gossips of Dorchester to capitalise on, titillating the inhabitants of a town long since renowned for its puritanical leanings, since the Reverend John White took Dorchester to task in the early 1600s. During the course of his spiritually influential 43-year Ministry, White actively sought to bring about a new social order and through his efforts Dorchester became known as a puritan town where existed a sober, godly, giving society; though perhaps not a *forgiving* society with regards to the transgressions of one 19-year-old girl, whose guilt to this day remains questionable.

Whether or not she was indeed one of those 'truly judged, or false, of doing to death their men', while Mary Channing has been assured a kind of grim celebrity – to quote Laurel Thatcher Ulrich , 'Well-behaved women seldom make history' – a certain measure of compelling sympathy for her case is nonetheless another lasting aspect of her legacy.

In view of the overly lengthy title of the 1706 publication previously given in full, henceforth where referred to throughout the text, the title of this publication will be abbreviated to *Serious Admonitions to Youth*. Any unattributed quotes in the following chapters have been drawn from this book.

Throughout, 'O.S.' denotes the old-style Julian calendar. The new style (N.S.) Gregorian calendar replaced the former Julian calendar in Catholic countries beginning in 1582, but was not adopted in England until 1752. Consequently, between 1582 and 1752, not only were two calendars in use in Europe (and in European colonies), but two different starts dates for the new year existed, both being in use in England. Although the 'Legal' year began on 25 March, the use of the Gregorian calendar by other European countries led to 1 January becoming commonly celebrated as New Year's Day and given as the first day of the year in almanacs. To avoid misinterpretation, both Old Style and New Style' dates were often used in England for dates falling between the new New Year (1 January) and the old New Year (25 March), a system known as 'double dating'. Such dates are usually shown by a slash mark [/] breaking the Old Style and New Style year, for example, the date of Mary Channing's execution is often given as 21 March 1705/6.

Chapter 1

'Spare the Rod... and spoil the Child'

Hudibras, Samuel Butler, 1662

T hough the poet and satirist Samuel Butler is the acknowledged coiner of this phrase, used in everyday speech to reinforce the now controversial belief that children will only flourish if chastised, physically or otherwise, for any wrongdoing, the notion is a much older one; a similar sentiment is expressed in the book of Proverbs, yet, judging from contemporary opinion, in respect of the proverbial rod, the parents of Mary Channing were found to be far too sparing.

If we accept the only existing contemporary account, which is sermonising to say the least, in her formative years, overindulgence seems to have been the detrimental hallmark of Mary's upbringing, influential upon her later character and subsequent behaviour as well as pivotal in the negative perceptions of her and indeed her ultimate fate. It may have been that she was merely the victim of judgemental condemnation for living her short life to the full. As to whether or not the questionable parenting skills of Richard and Elizabeth Brookes (variously spelt as Brooks and seemly varying at a whim) was the grounding for the development of their daughter's wayward inclinations, her apparent 'sluttishness', 'affected gaiety' and gaudiness was later to give way to vanity, promiscuity and rounds of riotous living. However, as the only daughter in a family of at least six brothers, (from her father's will we now know that Mary had six brothers that survived her – Richard, Caleb, William, Joshua, Ebenezer and Thomas) as no mention is made of any sisters in the account of her life, perhaps then her parents could be forgiven for spoiling their only daughter, perhaps in compensation for both parents' frequent absences from the family home. As they were busy managing properties and businesses in three counties, Mary would invariably have been deprived of the parental guidance and discipline of her parents. Growing up in a boisterous household shared with her brothers, in a climate of the business associated with her parents owning at least three inns or public houses in Dorchester, perhaps her high-spiritedness was a product of this domestic sphere. Again, Richard Brookes' will shows that he owned several properties in the town including an inn in the parish of Holy Trinity called the Royal Gate; another tenement in the parish of All Saints called the Beare. With her father branching out into business as a wagoner, certainly both parents were likely to have been preoccupied; with the additional management of properties in Somerset and Devon, a tenement and land at Honiton and land at Martock, Richard Brookes would have been called away for weeks, even months, at a time, leaving his wife to manage the businesses closer to home, as well as their large family. Thanks to their relative wealth, however, Mary's parents were in a position to indulge their only daughter materially, even if they did not have leisure in their busy lives to lavish time and attention on her.

Mary was born in Dorchester at the beginning of May 1687, in all probability in the fairly large house her parents owned in St Peter's parish, part of which was rented out. We know that the property was located on the north side of High East Street from the will of one of Mary's brothers, Caleb, who inherited the family home that was later known as the White Horse Inn. Reliance on the accuracy of Mary's date of birth, however, is based upon a line taken from the *Serious Admonitions to Youth*: 'I suppose there can be no mistake in this, because it came from her own mouth'. There is no baptismal record for Mary to back this up, as Richard and Elizabeth Brookes were both Anabaptists – a sect of religious separatists who did not believe in the baptism of infants. Holding the belief that infants were not punishable for sin because they had no awareness of good and evil and thus could not yet exercise free will, repent, and accept baptism, Anabaptists were baptised in adulthood, once education and life experience had enabled an individual to make an informed decision about their own faith. Mary herself was baptised as an adult into the established church while she was held in gaol awaiting her execution, the ceremony taking place on Sunday, 17 March 1705, a few weeks shy of her eighteenth birthday. As anyone practicing non-conformity at that time would have been frowned upon, the Brookes' religious leanings may well have been called into question with regard to the neglect in Mary's spiritual instruction, viewed as an essential discipline in any child's upbringing, in which they were so supposedly wanting. The author of *Serious Admonitions to Youth* was careful to point early on that her parents were negligent in the 'Improvements of a Religious Education' lacking 'a frequent and serious Inculcation of those Divine Truths'.

The Dorchester in which Mary was born had nevertheless been a focus for non-conformity; prior to this, however, it had remained a small market town since mediaeval times and, while population growth was slow, by the late seventeenth century, the population had expanded to an estimated 1,700 souls who occupied what was the former Roman frontier town of Durnovaria, its Roman origins still obvious in the vestiges of the amphitheatre known as Maumbury Rings to the south west of the town and from the pattern of the streets still following the line of Roman walls. In Hardy's day, he described the town viewed from the hills above as 'clean–cut and distinct, like a chessboard on a green table-cloth', and the remains of the ancient walls that once surrounded the town can still be seen today, though the majority have been replaced by pathways that form a square inside modern Dorchester known as The Walks. Laid out and planted with trees in the early eighteenth century, the better to satisfy the increasing genteel trend for the promenade, a small segment of the original Roman wall is still evident near the Top 'o Town roundabout at the western end of Dorchester's High Street. Dorchester also boasts the only example of a fully exposed Roman town house in the country, a survivor of the devolution of Roman Dorchester after the legions withdrew in the face of the fierce Saxon and Germanic raids which signalled the decline of the Empire, leaving the town all but abandoned save for a small number of people living inside the walls, grazing their cattle there and farming fields outside of the enclosure. By the time of the Norman Conquest, the population of Dorchester probably numbered several hundred, with cattle still grazing within the old Roman walls, but as time went by, people seem to have trickled back, so by the Medieval period, with three weekly markets, Dorchester had grown into a town again, with traders coming from all over Dorset to buy and sell at the four annual fairs – chiefly for cattle and sheep – also held there, close to the centre of town in a large field known as Fair Field on 14 February, Trinity Monday (a movable date following Trinity Sunday which falls on the Sunday after Whitsunday which itself is seven weeks after Easter Day!), 5 July and 5 August.

On through the Middle Ages, Dorchester remained small in comparison to the larger towns in England. Outside of London, the greatest centres of population were centred on the cathedral cities such as Lincoln, Canterbury, Chichester, York, Bath and Hereford; unlike all of its neighbouring counties, Dorset does not have a cathedral. By the year 1500, Dorchester was said to have 260 houses, which would put the estimated population at around one thousand. In spite of noted outbreaks of plague in 1563, 1579 and 1595 (after the latter epidemic is was said that Dorchester's living were insufficient to bury the dead) the population nevertheless climbed to the levels apparent in Mary's day, when, at the turn of the eighteenth century, at the centre of a wide rural area located on one of the busiest intersections in Dorset, Dorchester was then noted as one of the largest towns in the county.

The busy streets would have echoed with the shouts of itinerant trades-men calling for custom – knives to grind or milk fresh from the cow, their voices raised over the hubbub of gossips, beggars, shoppers, the harmonies of street-singers and the chiming of bells from church towers which all com-peted with the din of market carts and other horse-drawn traffic lumbering over the busy uneven roads, unpleasantly dusty in the hot summer months and virtually impassable in the winter, owing to their muddy conditions. Weary passengers travelling aboard the London Stage en route to Exeter would have disembarked at the King's Arms, on High East Street, just below Cornhill, after a two-and-a-half-day journey if they had joined the coach when it departed from the George Inn in Aldersgate, or just half a day if they had boarded the coach at the Plume of Feathers in Salisbury. Onward passengers for Exeter faced another day's travel, though in winter the prom-ised three-and-a-half-day journey from London to Exeter usually took six days. Amongst the foot traffic, sedan chairs wove their way up narrow streets and passageways as they conveyed wealthy occupants to their places of busi-ness, the less well-heeled pedestrians hurrying to and fro, picking their way between the open sewers which ran down the centre of the street, the gutters carrying away human waste and offal from butchers' stalls, as well as the tonnes of horse manure deposited daily on the thoroughfares.

Though the old street patterns persisted, the facade of Dorchester had been considerably altered over the years. The numerous Georgian build-ings still evident today, many faced in pale Portland stone, replaced those destroyed by the series of disastrous fires which Dorchester suffered in the seventeenth and eighteenth centuries. In 1613 the 'Great Fire', the precursor to its London namesake, destroyed much of the town. A candle-maker named Baker had accidentally spilt some boiling tallow at his workshop–home. As he had apparently made too large a fire under his melting-pot, assisted by a stiff breeze the blaze spread rapidly to the neighbouring wooden and thatched buildings in the tinder-dry conditions of that summer. It was said that 300 dwellings were destroyed, along with the two parish churches of All Saints and Holy Trinity, yet incredibly there was only one fatality, Cecily Bingham, the wife of a cobbler, who was burnt to death while trying to rescue a pair of shoes! Local industry seems to have been responsible for the other confla-grations afflicting the town, though of lesser severity: the fire in 1622 was started by a malster; the seat of the fire which broke out in 1725 was in a Brewhouse; while the blaze in 1775 was caused by a soap boiler – prudently –

and not before time – in 1776, thatched roofs were banned in Dorchester to reduce the risk of fire.

In spite of the candle-maker's clumsiness back in 1613, many viewed that particularly devastating conflagration as a sign from God, a 'fire from heaven', punishment for Dorchester's ungodly way of life. One of the strongest admonishers was the Reverend John White. A puritan divine and often called the 'Patriarch of Dorchester', though the Puritan movement became a major political force in England as a result of the English Civil War (1642–51), White had made his mark on the town prior to the political conflict that divided the country. While at the start of the seventeenth-century Dorchester was a small and not very distinguished market town, it was, however, the richest place in Dorset, partly due to the annual fairs. Into this perceived Sodom of the Stuart age walked the Reverend White in 1606 and his sermons made it very clear where he stood. When on 6 August 1613 the 'Great Fire' struck, this was interpreted by White, and others, as punishment direct from the Almighty for the townsfolk ungodly way of living and gave White the vital impetus behind his preaching and his sermons of repentance, in effect turning Dorchester into a bastion of puritanism.

Yet, even before White's time, Dorchester had been a place to which non-conformist religious sects had gravitated, hence the presence of Anabaptists in the community, like Mary's parents. Like Puritanism, the Anabaptist movement arose out of the Protestant Reformation, but Anabaptism was labelled as the 'Radical Reformation' of sixteenth-century Europe. Some have theorized that Anabaptists were actually the first Puritans since their reformed theology was being taught in the fifteenth century. The term Anabaptist however was not a denominational name, but a derisive term given to them because adherents re-baptized converts who had previously been baptized into the established church as infants.

Religious considerations were not only instrumental in effecting a change in the standing of Dorchester as a place of spiritual eminence, however, as one particular instance of intolerance demonstrated. In 1642, Hugh Green, a Catholic chaplain, was executed in the town, a victim of anti-Catholic persecution. After his horrifyingly botched execution, the mob, '… an ungodly multitude, from ten o'clock in the morning till four in the afternoon, stayed on the hill and sported themselves at football with his head.' In that same year, when the Civil War broke out, as a hotbed of Puritanism supporting Parliament, Dorchester was described as 'more against the King than any other place in England', 'a magazine from which other places were supplied with the principles of rebellion' and the town necessarily was one of the first places to be fortified against the Royalists. The military defences thrown up included those at Maumbury Rings, the earthworks of this once ancient Roman amphitheatre being re-modelled as an artillery fort guarding the town's southern approach. After the war however, and so pertinent to Mary's story, the entertaining role of the amphitheatre role was briefly revived; able to accommodate ten to twelve thousand spectators, where once the crowds had enjoyed Roman gladiatorial shows and sporting events and latterly in Medieval times entertainments such as bear-baiting and cock fights, at the turn of the eighteenth century, Dorchester's site of public execution was moved to Maumbury and again the Rings became a popular venue, though for 'hanging fairs', which continued to attract large crowds as a place of execution into the late 1700s.

Naturally, as Dorset's county town, Dorchester saw its fair share of public executions. And one such memorable event marking the town's history occurred less than two years before Mary's birth, when Judge Jeffreys descended upon Dorchester and held his Bloody Assize. Jeffreys was selected by James II to head the commission of Judges sent to the West Country in 1685 to punish those involved in the Monmouth Rebellion – an attempt to topple the Catholic James in favour the exiled Duke of Monmouth, the Protestant but illegitimate son of King Charles II, James II's brother and predecessor. During the Dorchester Assizes, a total of two hundred and ninety two prisoners were tried by the commission of Judges; of these, seventy four were executed in the town (though at Gallows Hill, at the end of the street now known as Icen Way, the former site of public executions before proceedings were moved to Maumbury Rings), while many of the remainder either died while languishing in prison of gaol fever – typhus – the remainder transported to plantations in the West Indies, which equated to a death sentence for many, facing long years of slavery in the colonies. The heads of some of the executed rebels were displayed on spikes outside St Peter's church, opposite the Judge's lodgings at 6 High West Street, an Elizabethan style house, now the aptly named Judge Jeffreys Restaurant. As Mary grew up, this is one of the buildings that would have been a familiar sight, along with the Antelope Hotel, just off the High Street where Jeffreys had held the assize trials in the Oak Room as, at the time, the local courtroom had fallen into disrepair, and its cells were being used to store gunpowder. Mary might even have been aware of the legendary tunnel recently uncovered beneath the now popular shopping thoroughfare of Antelope Walk, the passageway said to be wide enough for three judges to walk side by side, allowing them safe passage after delivering an unpopular verdict. It connected the lodgings in High West Street with the trial venue at the Antelope, now the Oak Room Tea Rooms.

While the old woollen industry upon which Dorchester's economy had depended was on the wane by the latter part of the seventeenth century, due to competition from northern towns, thanks to the town's growing brewing industry, Dorchester's prosperity grew and so too did the Brookes family business interests. Their relative wealth meant that Mary's parents were able to afford to give their daughter an education. Though women from even prosperous backgrounds received an inferior education to those of their male counterparts, Mary's parents were nevertheless keen that she be schooled to a level deemed suitable for a daughter of part of the aspiring commercial 'middle' class and taught to read and write '…to a proficiency deemed suitable for one of her sex', and Mary apparently excelled at her studies, which must have extended to learning Latin as, at her trial, after the indictment was read in English, she asked for it to be repeated in Latin before she made her plea. Thus spared the daily grind that was the fate of the majority of the population, the affluence of Mary's parents assured that she would never have to toil in the back-breaking servility of domestic service, one of the few employment options open to unmarried girls and young women in the late seventeenth century, born into less fortunate circumstances. Doubtless numbering amongst the Brookes household servants was at least one 'maid of all work', at the very bottom rung of the domestic ladder, working miserably long hours in return for the customary low wage paid for unskilled housework and doubtless waiting on Mary hand and foot. Having lit the fire in Mary's bedroom before she awoke, emptying her chamber pot and staggering back with buckets filled from the nearest pump with water to heat ready for Mary's ablutions and for general cleaning and washing, she probably would have spent half her day carrying pails up and down stairs. This was just the beginning of the laborious repetitive tasks that were the pattern of a servant's day. While her mistress pondered whether her new gown would look best trimmed with lace or ribbons, it was the servant who was left to do the stitching and to launder it after the hem had been soiled by the filthy streets.

Certainly, social status was the prevalent and dominant aspect of the times and played a key role as a distinguishing feature in early-modern English society. Social hierarchy determined everything about a person and was instrumental in shaping their entire lives. For centuries, the aristocracy had been the most powerful section of British society, but increasingly in the seventeenth and eighteenth centuries wealth became a determining influence on social rank. The status of the merchant class improved as people saw that trade was a progressively vital part of the country's wealth. And with land no longer the only source of wealth, the emerging 'middle classes' became more respected, growing in power and confidence. At the beginning of the eighteenth century, those stepping up onto the new rung of the social ladder accounted for about fifteen per cent of the population – the upper middle class including certain professionals and merchants, while the lower middle classes included artisans, shopkeepers and tradesmen, as well as proprietors of taverns, such as Mary's father. A tavern was distinguished from a public ale house by dint of being run as a private enterprise, where drinkers were 'guests' rather than members of the public, and therefore a step up. However, in attempting to move up the social scale and attain some form of wealth and class, these men and women were often ridiculed for their lack of social graces. Even though the Brookes family were successful in their business enterprises and would have been considered quite wealthy by the standards of the day, they certainly would not have moved in the same social circles as the gentry. From the sixteenth century, in a relatively rural location such as Dorchester, there would have been quite a gulf between the likes of the farming yeomanry and tradesmen, and those occupying the social echelon above them. It was therefore vital to families such as the Brooks to strive and make every effort to conform to and mirror the social niceties of the cultural elite, the betterment of themselves demonstrated to best advantage in the upbringing and development of their children. Consequently, in a bid to prepare Mary for presentation into polite society and the better to prepare her for an advantageous marriage, her parents sought to further add to their daughter's social finish and desirability by sending her for dancing lessons, then seen as one of the fashionable accomplishments of a refined young lady. As well as the consideration of the social prestige conferred by a 'good' marriage, as it was a very difficult thing for women to find ways of making an independent living, securing a husband was a matter of great importance, and a suitable husband at that. Accordingly, every fortnight, Mary attended a local dance school in Dorchester. As well as a proficiency in music, drawing and languages, dancing was one of those social graces that was supposedly the mark and birthright of the polite world. While the fundamental purpose of the dancing master was in the tutoring of the graceful tread of the Minuet and other formal dances of the era, along with some of the more robust yet socially acceptable variations of popular English Country dances, as mastery of these steps was a necessary prelude to the ballroom, the additional coaching he provided in etiquette, in deportment and in the cultivation of that air of relaxed assurance so much admired as one of the social mores of the age was essential. After all, clumsiness equated with boorishness, vulgarity, rusticity, bad manners and bad taste. Graceful manners and agreeable address ranked among the most reliable indicators of good breeding and, according to the 1711 edition of the *Spectator* published in May of that year it was 'the proper Business of a Dancing-Master to regulate these Matters'.

However, while the aim was to add to Mary's finesse, and polish her manners – Richard Brookes was sure to expect a return for the money he was laying out for his daughter's dance tuition – the plan backfired as, after being drilled in the Baroque and the Allemande, the dance classes that she so judiciously attended provided the vivacious young Mary with the opportunity to exploit her new found liberty. Revelling in the company of the new friends she had made, she 'began to delight too much in the vanities of entertainment' and after the classes were over, in the absence of their instructor, who had presumably left with a copy of *The English Dancing Master* tucked under his arm, the fun could really begin, with an opportunity for nights of frivolity and mirth with her other young friends being something which Mary unquestioningly exploited.

At this stage, to what degree Mary's parents were aware of their daughter's developing wayward inclinations we cannot know. They were obviously aware that she was a high-spirited girl, but their own preoccupations may have smothered any niggling concerns they may have had. Yet they clearly took the view that the climate of pastoral simplicity and rusticity of late seventeenth-century Dorset was not one which afforded the opportunities necessary to equip a young lady for the niceties of high society, and they saw fit to send her off on visits to Exeter and London, their intention being to 'reduce her rather rude and unpolished carriage into a decent comeliness' and give her 'a wider experience of the world' – presumably they felt that these were qualities in which their daughter was still distinctly lacking. Mary needed next to no encouragement. Of course, the social scene in London was unrivalled, being set in the largest, most commercialized and industrialized city in England at the time. Roughly half a million citizens called London their home at the beginning of the eighteenth century, making for an eclectic mix. The noble and the destitute all walked the same streets, made atrociously filthy by the dirty water systematically dumped from upper windows along with horse manure and human waste, yet those who visited the city for the first time, mingling with the wealthy, as well as the beggars, prostitutes and pickpockets, were still overawed and mesmerised by the capital. With entertainments ranging from theatres, inns and pleasure gardens, to shops displaying the latest fashions, even the exotic was available – by 1700, you could buy a pineapple on the quays, at a price of course. Yet Exeter also had its attractions and with her father's business connections in Honiton, a visit to Exeter could be even more easily arranged than a jaunt to London. In 1698, the travel writer Celia Fiennes, who famously embarked on a horse-back tour around England, wrote that:

'... the prospect of ye Citty of Exeter was very pleasant ... a town very well built. The streets are well-paved, spacious streets and a vast trade is carried on ... This City does exceedingly resemble London for, besides these buildings I mentioned for the several Markets, there is an Exchange full of shops like our Exchanges are, only its but one walk along as was the Exchange at Salisbury House in the Strand; there is also a very large space railed in just by the Cathedral, with walks round it'.

Yet both Celia and Mary must have had a mind as to where they stepped if they enjoyed such walks, as Exeter was equally subject to the same levels of filth and dirt, though the extent of the general pollution not as great as those experienced in the capital, where it was sometimes necessary for candles to be lit at midday in busy shops owing to the smoggy conditions outside. Many travellers to London also noted the smell of the city as they approached from far away; letters received from the capital were often said to have a 'sooty' odour, a similar problem with noisome bouquet still appar-ent in Exeter in 1799, with one writer, a Spanish visitor, commenting that the town:

'... is an ancient city, and has been so slow in adopting the modern improvements [i.e. paving and the cleaning of streets] that it has the unsavoury odour of Lisbon. One great street runs through the city from East to West. The rest consists of dirty lanes. The streets are not flagged neither are they regularly cleaned as in other parts of the kingdom.'

And while the same commentator held that Exeter 'cannot be compared with Seville, or Cordova, or Burgos' he nevertheless recommended Exeter as 'yet certainly it is a noble pile'. And Exeter's burgeoning status as a 'large rich, beautiful, populous' city having recovered from after the ravages of the Civil War had been further alluded to earlier in the eighteenth century by Daniel Defoe, who, on his journey round Great Britain, on arriving in Exeter described it as a place 'that 'tis full of gentry, and good company'. Needless to say, wherever Mary was whipped around in the social whirl, enjoying the entertainments that either London or Exeter had to offer, she would doubtless have been fashionably attired – and we can assume that this was a young lady who enjoyed wearing whatever was the latest trend.

As far as fashionable dress was concerned, it was the mantua which dominated the beginning of the eighteenth century, to the extent that dressmakers were called 'mantua makers'. France had always been the arbiter of fashion, and indeed, the name mantua comes from the French word *'manteau'*, meaning coat. Introduced in the late seventeenth century as a casual dress alternative to the heavily structured court dress required by the French king Louis XIV, the mantua was initially more of a robe than a dress, later becoming a more formal gown, with the bodice taking on new importance as a place of opulent display, with the fashionable attachment of the 'stomacher', an inverted triangle of richly embroidered fabric. The placement of the stomacher atop the increasingly full skirts of the mantua, usually worn over a petticoat, which was visible under the front opening of the gown, created a narrow-waisted silhouette. While the stomacher could be made from the same matching fabric as the mantua, often highly decorated fabrics of a contrasting colour were worn, increasing the opportunity for additional show as well as laces and ruffles added to the elbow length sleeves of the gown. Thus attired, Mary, presumably shod in the latest satin, stylishly heeled shoes would have stepped out on the town, though if she was not wearing pattens – protective wooden soled overshoes – she may well have flagged down a passing Sedan chair to avoid the omnipresent filth of the streets spoiling her smart footwear. She might also have applied cosmetics in order to complete the popular look of the day, which according to a remark made by Lady Mary Wortley Montagu was that 'All the ladies have … snowy foreheads and bosoms, jet eyebrows and scarlet lips …' While false eyebrows made from mouse skin were sometimes worn and the scarlet lips alluded to achieved with the application of garish vermillion lip rouge, the essential pale pallor was accomplished with the lavish use of the 'designer' yet toxic white lead based face powders which contained cerussite, once the key ingredient in now banned lead based paints. While the inherent detrimental effects to health were obvious, the use of lead based cosmetics continued well into the nineteenth century, with the pursuit of the socially elitist ideal of a fairer than fair complexion; for one dedicated follower of fashion the 'dead white' look proved literally fatal. Maria Gunning, Countess of Coventry was a society hostess and celebrated beauty of her day and certainly a victim of vanity. Maria died, aged twenty-seven in 1760, her lovely face eaten away by the ravages of the lead-based make-up she insisted on plastering on daily, the cumulative effect of repeated applications of these poisonous cosmetics eventually resulting in horrific disfigurement and death. Mary's own youthful complexion may have been fresh enough not to require any heavy coverage, but she might have indulged in the application of the flirtatious facial embellishment of patches, worn by both men and women to conceal blemishes and scars. By the early 1700s, however, beauty patches had become such a cosmetic staple that they were worn more for aesthetic accent than blemish camouflage. Made from tiny pieces of black velvet, silk or taffeta – though if you were restricted to the economy range you might have to make do with mouse skin, as employed in the manufacture of the aforementioned false eyebrows – patches were available in a myriad of pre-cut shapes from stars, diamonds, crescent moons and even tiny horse-drawn carriages. Affixed with a mixture of glycerin and other ingredients including extract of sturgeon swim-bladder, the emerging language of patch symbolism blossomed, with, for instance, a patch placed above the lip meaning coquetry; on the forehead, grandeur; and at the corner of an eye, passion. We can imagine Mary being on trend, and to coin a contemporary term, she would have been a regular Pink of the Fashion, perhaps even disparaged as a 'Bartholomew Baby', another eighteenth-century slang term, for a person dressed in a tawdry manner, like the dolls or 'babies' sold at Bartholomew Fair, one of London's pre-eminent summer events.

Yet in spite of her appearance, Mary's Dorset accent, with the characteristic rhotic 'r's pronounced after a vowel, must have marked her out as a provincial visitor, though to a lesser extent in Exeter, where the variations in the West Country dialect would have been no stranger to the local ear. This would have been clear signifier of class distinction; no amount of ruffles or ribbons could disguise Mary's rustic roots, so perhaps she made an effort to rub off her rural vernacular by linguistically mimicking the speech patterns of her rather more cosmopolitan social superiors. Though Received Pronunciation (RP), which emerged from the eighteenth and nineteenth aristocracy only became a dogma in the late nineteenth century, fostered by the public school system, nevertheless, a strong sense of correct pronunciation was well established by Shakespeare's day. Linguist John Honey suggests that the bard 'grew up speaking the Stratford-upon-Avon variant of the Warwickshire dialect' – but he would have had to modify his speech in order to get on in the world. Regional accents have been noticed, especially where they might not be expected, for centuries. Sir Walter Raleigh's West Country vowels stood out at the Elizabethan and Jacobean courts, while Sir Robert Walpole, Britain's first and longest serving prime minister, in office from 1721-42, spoke all his life with the accent of a Norfolk squire, being constantly derided for this and other failures of refinement by his 'better-spoken' contemporaries. And with regard to Mary's Dorset dialect, the strong idea of the proper English accent, which above all must not be provincial, was one that mattered to Thomas Hardy; though his literature drew immeasurably on his 'Wessex' origins, not to mention Mary as his poetical muse, he was nonetheless ashamed of the thick Dorset accents of both his siblings.

However, while the ultimate aim of these trips away from home was one of personal improvement and genteel sophistication, removed from the reach of parental supervision, such that it was, Mary developed not so much 'poise' but rather a propensity to take pleasure in less than refined company. On her return to Dorchester, having discovered 'delight in company', her licence to take up with her former acquaintances was renewed with vigour and 'she could not be made to forsake it'. No longer restricted to the fortnightly irregularity of indulging in frivolity after dance classes, Mary took to nightly meetings of intemperate revelry in neighbours' houses, evenings frittered away in gay abandon, and, while initially Mary partied with friends of her own age and sex, inevitably the evenings were increasingly spent in the company of 'gentlemen'.

It would also seem that 'being now of an Age fit to receive the Impressions of Love' Mary was enjoying the attentions of an admirer. We can assume that the pairing was in its truest sense as in describing Mary's paramour as a 'lover' the *Serious Admonitions to Youth* was employing the use of the word in its sexual context; of course, the sexual meaning of 'love' was present from the very beginnings of Old English, but it was not until the late seventeenth century that the term implied a specific sexual element, inferring an illicit partnership, or even sexual intercourse itself. Though the identity of her 'lover' is unknown, he was amongst those young neighbours she had met at one of the nightly debauches held at a friend's house. However, the couple latterly took to meeting at public houses in Dorchester, though to avoid parental censure we can presume not in any of the Brookes family-owned inns; their assignations possibly took place in the Olde Ship Inn, the oldest pub in Dorchester built around 1600, or at the Antelope Hotel, the Ship's great rival house, or perhaps the George or the Green Dragon. In such establishments, as Mary's teenage infatuation grew, keen to retain her sweetheart's affections at any cost, literally, she would happily foot the bill for evenings spent entertaining him with 'wine, and whatever else she thought would please', Mary 'gladly paying the whole charge for the sake of his company'. In a further demonstration of her love, Mary showered her swain with costly gifts, including fashionable ruffles and cravats (the designer accessory of their day), one of which made of lace and flourished with gold would certainly have left Mary out of pocket. She may even have laid out for the purchase of love charms (or even rudimentary contraceptives – a matter which will be discussed in a later chapter) from a 'cunning person' or folk healer, often consulted to cast spells or charms, to tell a person's fortune, divine the name of their future love – a great favourite with teenage girls – or ensure a loved one's fidelity.

As well as the excessive expenses Mary ran up on lavish gifts and entertaining, this was not her only outlay. She was also giving items of value in payment to those who allowed the use of their homes as a private meeting place for her and her young man. In no time, the cost began to tell and Mary (in collusion with some of her closest friends) turned to theft, even from her own parents, in order to finance and maintain her profligate lifestyle. While Mary's assignations were ostensibly secret, the censorious townsfolk of Dorchester soon got wind of the fact that Mary was 'not living within the bounds of modesty'.

At this point, we have to credit some of Mary's friends with a measure of probity, some of them expressing their misgivings at the possible ramifications of Mary's conduct. The concerned efforts on their part, however, proved ineffectual. Word was certainly getting around, reaching many ears, and Mary was even approached by one of the town's preachers who, having known Mary for many years, presumably since childhood, remonstrated with her about the consequences of leading such a dissipated life. Did she not realise 'the folly of attempting to conceal her ill practices by lying pretenses, and the calamities they must bring upon her'? Mary did not respond well to these strictures, resenting being told that she should give 'some serious thoughts of her condition, and to live a more regular and unblameable life' and reacted as any angry adolescent might, with vehement self-justification. Though the preacher continued to press his point, Mary's temper eventually cooled and, thanking him for his concern, she assured him that she herself placed no value on the common disapproval of her conduct as she had nothing to reproach herself for; though she loved her young man she had never given him any presents, and we can read into this a further denial of any improper behaviour, backed up by her oath by that if what she had said were untrue she hoped 'she might never enter the Kingdom of Heaven'. Whether Mary was deriving some irreverent satisfaction from being deceitful, lying to cover her tracks and hoping to damp down the increasing heat of local gossip, her denial was transparent to her admonisher and, though he made further appeals that Mary more seriously consider her situation, in an act of defiance, she increased her pleasure-seeking and began to consort openly with several other young men in the town. Throughout, she was still attending the dancing school that met every fortnight and, once the lessons had ended, there was ample opportunity for an attractive and vivacious young woman like Mary to beguile any number of young beaux to keep her company into the early hours.

Taking 'her greater fill of pleasure' still further, throwing herself headlong into Dorchester's social scene, Mary's next endeavour was to attend every one of the private balls thrown in the town. Though anyone who paid for a ticket could attend an assembly ball, the most exciting events in provincial life, private balls, tended to be rather grander affairs and entry to these lavish and exclusive events was by invitation only. Though codes of behaviour were exacting, the combination of proprietary and stifled passion made such occasions the stage for a heady kind of courtship. In a crowded room, lit by candles and often overwhelmingly hot, there was the opportunity for flirtation and dancing with a variety of partners and, though both men and women wore gloves throughout, couples performing together in close physical proximity, while being observed by others, made for a sexually charged atmosphere. Those not dancing might play at cards in an adjacent room (a proper private ball would have tables laid out for Basset or Faro) and with the constant, copious flow of wine, punch and other intoxicating drinks served on such occasions, the inexperienced and inebriated invariably gambled and lost more than they could afford, the availability of alcohol likewise fuelling the antics of those of an excitable nature.

Entertainment was now Mary's sole *raison d'être* and, not to be outdone, she threw a ball of her very own. Bestowing generous gifts on her guests, Mary managed to conceal the arrangements (and the cost) from her parents by holding the event in another gentlewoman's house in the town, no doubt opportunely timed to coincide with one of her father's frequent absences and capitalising on her mother's preoccupation with running the household and various businesses while he was away. Indeed, Elizabeth Brookes must have been considerably distracted as she failed to notice the various occasions when Mary frequently entertained friends in the family home. On the rare occasions that Mrs Brookes did come upon one of her daughter's parties, the wine, punch and the more costly fare laid out was hastily removed; to all intents and purposes, as far as Mary's mother was concerned, her daughter was merely returning the kind and innocent hospitality of her friends. The pseudo-sedate gatherings outside of the family home also provided a useful cover for Mary's absences when trysting with her lover; ostensibly she enjoying the reciprocal hospitality of the guests welcomed into the Brookes' parlour. These deceptions, however, made some of those friends uneasy and reluctant to accept her invitations. Yet Mary continued and forced the merriment on them, intent that nothing should curtail the 'sensual life' to which she was now accustomed.

Of course, gossip was inescapable. Singing loud from the Devil's songsheet, Mary's nightly cavorting became the talk of Dorchester. It was inevitable that, in a town renowned for its sanctimonious standards ever since the Reverend John White had striven to turn Dorchester into a Godly town governed by the principles of the Christian faith, it would have been difficult for any parent, especially those heavily involved with the community through business, to turn a deaf ear to the slights and slurs concerning their daughter's unseemly behaviour. Yet, while Richard and Elizabeth Brookes seemed to have been deaf to the whispers of depravity, even the most credulous of parents could not ignore the letter of complaint penned by the puritanical hand of one who was not even an acquaintance of the family. Incensed by the impropriety of the gatherings which Mary frequented, at which 'too much noise' was made to keep the affairs private – we can imagine the peals of laughter carried on the night air as the sated company sprawled amongst empty bottles – the officious gentlemen drove his sentiment home first by messenger to the Brookes' house, followed up by a strongly worded letter. Still Mary's parents refused to believe the licentious allegations levelled against their only daughter, dismissive of the complaints about Mary's outrageous conduct and disruptive entertainments, until, that was, the eventual scandal attached to her name became so great that not even Richard and Elizabeth Brookes could remain in denial; the sharp tongues of the gossips cut deep.

Chapter 2

Mrs Channing

As Mary's extravagant behaviour and want of propriety increased, there were those amongst her friends (probably those same friends who had previously expressed their misgivings) who, increasingly concerned at the consequences of her excesses, decided it was time to enlighten her parents as to the true nature of their daughter's frequent nightly debauches. Made aware of the extent to which his daughter's life was 'chiefly spent in Pleasure', the reprimands of Mary's father were nevertheless met with scant regard. And her mother's remonstrations, such as they were, she being described as apparently of 'a quite different temper' clearly had little influence over Mary's continuing outrageous behaviour. It was clear that if their daughter's character, as well as the standing of the family, were not to be irreparably tarnished then something must be done to curb the wayward Mary Brookes.

In the circumstances, finding Mary a husband seemed the best available option, and, in accordance with the seventeenth century aphorism 'marry thy daughters betimes [that is, early] lest they marry themselves', Mary's parents decided to 'dispose of her in Marriage as soon as possible', in the hopes that perhaps a husband would exercise more control over her than they had been able. In seventeenth century England and beyond, a woman was regarded as the 'weaker vessel', a phrase taken from the New Testament, a creature supposedly physically, intellectually, morally and even spiritually inferior to a man; therefore, the man had a right to dominate her. At the time, the status of a married woman also conferred a sense of sexual integrity and respectability, as well as a measure of social prestige; in Mary's case, that was clearly just what was needed. And besides, the binding state of matrimony was one that every girl was expected to dutifully accept if she were to fulfil her role in society, especially in a society so strongly influenced by Puritan values, and especially in a town such as Dorchester with its strong puritanical connections.

Thus began the search for a suitable spouse and to sweeten the prospect of taking his daughter's hand in marriage, Richard Brookes made it known that whomsoever took her as a wife would be the better for a 'considerable fortune', offered as dowry - when entering into marriage, women were usually given a lump sum of money or a part of their parents' estate as a dowry. The lure, not surprisingly, encouraged several would-be suitors to 'make their addresses'; however, in spite of the financial incentive and Mary's apparent beauty – she was described as a handsome young woman 'of good natural parts' – the detriment attached to her reputation however must have been far reaching, as none of the potential candidates could 'be prevailed on' to take Mary's hand, until, that was, a young man named Thomas Channing began to pay court to Miss Brookes. Having recently completed his apprenticeship (his father had established a grocer's shop in Dorchester for Thomas to run), he was now, at the age of twenty-five, at a point in his life where he was expected to marry and settle down. Thomas' background, respectability and future prospects made him an ideal choice in the eyes of any would-be in-laws, never mind those who were looking to off-load a flighty daughter and besides, Mary had no choice in the matter. The cultural pressure to respect one's elders and to submit and obey their commandments was ubiquitous; absolute obedience to one's parents and social superiors was fundamental, instilled from the earliest age and extended to even the most wilful of daughters.

Hailing from Maiden Newton, a parish eight miles north-west of Dorchester, the Channing family actually came from the small hamlet of Cruxton, situated just south of the town, close to the River Frome. One Richard Channing, Gentleman, was recorded as the owner of Higher 'Crookston' (an archaic spelling of Cruxton) in 1654 and the Channings were known to have still been at the family property in 1743. Clearly, the Channings were a family of local standing in Maiden Newton, which in Thomas' day was a larger settlement, having had its own market and fair from the time of Henry III; the remains of the old Market Cross, dating to the fifteenth century, still stands at the junction of Dorchester Road and Church Road. The second of seven children born to Richard Channing by his wife Elizabeth Bartlett, Thomas was baptised at Mappowder in Dorset on 3 June 1679. His mother was from Plush, a little over three miles from Mappowder where Thomas' parents had married and it was normal for the wife to return to her home parish for the birth of their earlier children because of the risks attendant on pregnancy. This meant that he was eight years older than Mary and, while contemporary moralists recommended that a couple contemplating marriage should be of a similar age as a determining factor in deciding whether a match was 'appropriate', in this case the age difference was not significant enough to daunt Mary's parents, who eagerly 'pressed for the match'.

As well as the concerns over age difference, those same contemporary moralists also advocated in their marital advice that as well as being of similar background, financial circumstances and religious beliefs, it was beneficial for a husband and wife to respect and like one another, but that any overt initial sexual attraction should be dismissed in favour of seeking 'inner qualities'. It was considered that passionate love alone was a bad grounding for marriage, as the heat of love would soon cool; in such circumstances, families may have considered thwarting an imprudent union in the best possible interests of ensuring an individual's future happiness. There were no grounds for this last concern on Thomas Channing account however. Though on paper he presented an eminently eligible catch, he was never a likely candidate to inflame Mary's desires. Unfortunately, Thomas' physical appearance was less than perfect ... Though not every girl could expect an Adonis to be selected as her husband, the entry in the *Newgate Calendar* (for the erroneously spelt case of Mary 'Channel') made note that Thomas Channing:

> 'had nothing to recommend him but his wealth, which was as much superior to the rest of her suitors as his person was inferior to them: his limbs and body were in some measure ill proportioned, and his features in no wise agreeable; but what rendered him the more detestable and ridiculous in her [Mary's] sight was his splay-foot, which did not in the least concur with her sublime and lofty temper.'

Judging by the description of Mary herself in the same entry, 'Being now in the flower of her youth and bloom of her beauty,' looks-wise she was clearly out of Thomas' league and besides, with her affections engaged elsewhere, understandably she could scarcely be persuaded to be civil to her intended, let alone rejoice in the prospect of his becoming her husband. She declared in company that:

> '... if her Father forc'd her to Marry any Person contrary to her Inclinations, she would make him a Cuckold, and wish'd some dreadful Calamity might befall her if ever she Marry'd Mr. Channing'.

Prophetic words indeed ...

While Thomas Channing may not have been the most appealing choice of life partner, or even dance partner for that matter, with his flattened, turned-out foot, he nevertheless had feelings and could not fail to be acutely aware of the contempt in which Mary held him, perhaps understandably in the face of her all too apparent derision, Thomas himself now began to say that he would not have Mary. Presumably, in spite of his physical detractions, his wealth and prospects were ample attraction to tempt other young ladies and he turned his attentions to another prospective bride for a time. But the steely resolve of Mrs Brookes was not to be subverted and, intent on securing Mr Channing as husband for her daughter, after some sharp reprimands – especially after Elizabeth Brookes became aware of the extent of her daughter's extravagances and the methods she had used to obtain the money to finance them, namely the shameful theft from her own parents – Mary was confined to her chamber for several days, held under a kind of house arrest, or, to use modern terminology, she was 'grounded'. Left alone to sulk, deprived of all pleasurable entertainment and the immodest company she had become accustomed to, eventually, for the sake of her liberty, Mary grudgingly agreed to marry Thomas Channing. This decision may have been swayed, however, by the prospect of freedom from parental control, as well as gaining immediate, and potentially lasting, emancipation.

Though Mary had consented to matrimony, she had no intention of spending the rest of her days as Mrs Channing. No sooner was she released from her confinement, after her supposed acquiescence to her parents' plans, she contrived to elope and wed her former lover – persuading a close friend to act as her intermediary. Perhaps before all the business of finding her a husband had gathered momentum, Mary's lover himself may have even promised her marriage. However, if the pledge had been made, it proved hollow and Mary's chagrin must have been unimaginable when she learned of that young man's crushing response in flatly refusing to carry through the proposal. It was now clear that Mary was out of options, though a silver-lining presented itself in the possibility that even though she would be bound to the undesirable Thomas Channing, he might yet prove to be the kind of husband who could be governed and manipulated.

For the majority, in Mary's day, the oppressive and restrictive status of women was the norm. Confined to traditional gender roles, frequently the chief consideration for a man in his choice of wife was her ability to run an efficient household. Indeed 'helpmate' was a term that the Puritans liked to use when referring to a 'good wife', representative of a society which forced women to remain in the domestic or private sphere, subject to the societal system of patriarchy evolved as the primary way to regulate women's behaviour and maintain social control – an aspect of the perceived gender equilibrium that will be explored in a later chapter – there were however exceptions. Not all women were accepting of being bent to the supreme dominance of patriarchy – and Mary was such a one.

It was generally accepted that the position of a wife was dictated by the patriarchal nature of family relationships, with the emphasis on the subordination of women. Common Law was heavily biased in the favour of the husband; as well as the fact that a married woman had no financial rights independent of her husband, he also had the right to beat his wife, Mary must nevertheless have been reasonably confident that she had the measure of Thomas Channing, agreeing to enter into what was, for the vast majority of men and women in late seventeenth-century England and for at least two centuries thence, an indissoluble union representing a lifelong commitment. Legal divorce was a lengthy and costly procedure which discriminated against women. Informal separations or desertions were socially frowned upon and were often economically disadvantageous. Yet Mary must have viewed the marriage as a way of 'having her cake and eating it', with the *Serious Admonitions to Youth* noting that doubtless 'the Devil might form in her some Designs, of spending her future Life in an uncontroul'd State of Pleasure'.

Clearly, Mary's parents were keen to capitalise on their daughter's eventual voluntary consent, so, before she had a change of heart, the very next day following her decision, Thomas Channing was summoned back to the Brookes' house there to be entertained by a refreshingly compliant Mary whose pleasant and attentive demeanour masked her true contempt; a commendable performance on the part of one who only days before had 'expressed an Uneasiness in his [Thomas'] Company' but who now would not hear of her prospective bridegroom leaving until 'their marriage was agreed on to be in two days time'.

With seemingly indecent haste, the marriage was arranged for Sunday, 14 January 1705. However, despite the short notice, the day of the ceremony was postponed by Thomas Channing. Whether he began to have serious misgivings about his choice (as we shall see, the lack of Channing parental blessing may have been a contributory factor), or he simply got 'cold feet', we do not know. In turn, for her part Mary was also having second thoughts, she beginning to 'show an unwillingness to proceed farther'. Here again Mrs Brookes stepped in, resolving 'to have it done'. At a meeting held later that evening at her brother's house, Mary was 'prevailed upon to continue in her Resolution of Marriage', the line of her mother's persuasive argument being that the probability of a happily married life with Mary's former lover (Mrs Brookes was clearly unaware of that young man's refusal of Mary's prior clandestine proposal) was far outweighed by the certainty and security that matrimony with Thomas Channing would bring. His father after all owned 'a plentiful estate' and Thomas himself was already settled into a good trade which promised a sufficient income and a secure, if not felicitous, future.

With both parties seemingly reconciled and allowing no time to further rue their choice, or the consequences, the mis-matched couple were privately married at a neighbouring church the following Monday morning, 15 January. Mary was still 18 years old at the time, Thomas aged 25. The timing of the wedding may also however have been influenced by the government-declared 'day of fasting' set for 19 January that year, in atonement for the 'crying sins of this nation' seen as the impetus for God's punishment sent in the form of the 'Great Storm', the week-long hurricane that struck the south of England and the English Channel in November the previous year. The unprecedented ferocity and duration of this storm was generally reckoned by witnesses as beyond anything in living memory. The winds that tore across the country sent the roofs of houses flying, levelled barns and knocked flat thousands of trees; it was reported that 4,000 oaks perished in the New Forest alone. In London, approximately 2,000 massive chimney stacks were blown down and, as the lead roofing was being peeled off Westminster Abbey, Queen Anne had to shelter in a cellar at St James's Palace to avoid collapsing chimneys and part of the roof. At Wells however, Bishop Richard Kidder and his wife were not so fortunate, being killed when two chimney stacks in the palace fell on them while they were asleep in their bed. Yet the cost in lives was especially great to those at sea – ships overtaken by the gale were wrecked and sunk and the loss of life was estimated at 8,000 men – one ship was even found driven fifteen miles inland.

On the day of the wedding, as she was given away by her father, Richard Brookes could not have foreseen the havoc that would be wrought by the tempestuous nature of his own daughter; presumably he was as relieved as his wife, who looking on who must have supposed that all their concerns would now be allayed by the disposal of Mary in matrimony. We can imagine that while Mary may not have worn a smile on her face she was at least dressed in her finest. While it is commonly supposed that Queen Victoria was responsible for the introduction and subsequent enduring popularity of the white wedding dress, long before Victoria, white was a popular choice for brides, at least for those who could afford it. In accordance with the presumption that love would bloom after a marriage, romance certainly took a backseat at weddings and the bride's dress was just another excuse to show the wealth and culture of her family, as before the invention of effective bleaching techniques, white was a valued colour, both difficult to achieve and hard to maintain. Those brides married in white were demonstrating their family's wealth, not their purity as is so often misattributed. This would certainly have been missing the mark if indeed Mary did wear white on her wedding day!

As to the 'neighbouring church' the Channings emerged from as husband and wife – did they both force expressions of jocularity one has to wonder – unfortunately as there is no existing record of their nuptials, we must rely on supposition to point to the likeliest candidate in which the ill-fated union was celebrated. St Peter's seems the most probable choice; one of the three main parish churches in Dorchester, along with Holy Trinity and All Saints (All Saints was also referred to as 'Alhalens' or 'All Hallows'), St Peter's was and is the largest and the principal church in the town. We know that Mary and Thomas were not married in Holy Trinity as marriage registers for this church and for the period in question have survived and been transcribed. Though there is a gap in the All Saints register between 1703-1711, the Reverend Hutchens, who will appear later in Mary's story, though living at his curacy of Bradford Peverell at the time of the wedding also recorded some of the marriages celebrated at All Saints, yet as the Channing marriage was not listed in either the All Saints or the Bradford Peverell register or for that matter elsewhere in Dorset amongst the wealth of online ancestry resources now available to the researcher, we must rely on conjecture. The conspicuous missing entries from the transcription of marriage registers for St Peter's Dorchester between August 1704 and May 1706 are quite easily explained. The incumbent rector at the time, the Reverend Samuel Reyner, had died aged 81 on 11 October 1704 – certainly a ripe old age for the times – three months prior to Thomas and Mary's marriage. His replacement did not fill the vacant post until 17 March 1705, so this would account for the absence of any record of the Channing's marriage, which in all likelihood was celebrated in St Peter's.

Wherever they were wedded, the knot was now tied, though how securely (or otherwise) was soon to become apparent. No sooner had the 'happy' couple returned home than a wedding party that was to last two days ensued. After the ceremony, the rest of the day and evening were given over to dancing 'and all sorts of Mirth' – presumably Thomas, inhibited by his flattened foot was side-lined from the cavorting. That must have pleased the bride. With invitations extended to Mary's former friends and neighbours of both sexes, whose company she had so much enjoyed, and with the news of her marriage celebration spreading throughout the town, the festivities became something of a public affair, marked by Mary showing scant affection for her new husband whom she publicly ridiculed. By the early hours, with the revelries finally winding down, some of the guests were invited to stay the night, presumably participating in the 'Bedding ritual', a ceremony common in eighteenth century Europe in which newlyweds were put to bed together and toasted by their attendants. Sometimes the bed was blessed; sometimes, a more intimate, inner circle of friends even stayed to witness the consummation, confirming the legality of the marriage – this was clearly not the case on Mary's wedding night however as, on joining her husband in the marital bed, Mary promptly turned her back on him with 'scornful disdain' and could not be persuaded to change her posture despite the repeated entreaties of some of her ribald friends.

After this humiliating start to his married life, Thomas Channing's sufferings were to continue throughout the next day, passed in a similarly raucous manner. Needless to say, those same ravenous gossips who had feasted on tales of Mary's nightly romps in her single state were now fed by tales of the impropriety of her wedding celebrations, not to mention the insinuations of the rather hasty and secretive arrangement and celebration of the marriage in the first place. Added to which, there was the censure of the frivolous conduct of Mrs Brookes; Mary's mother gave 'wedding favours' to virtually everyone in town, then later refused to foot the bill for the cost of her own extravagances.

Though the wedding and subsequent shenanigans were the talk of Dorchester, Thomas Channing's parents seemed wholly unaware of what had gone on – obviously they were not present at the hurriedly arranged wedding and certainly not amongst the hard-core of reception guests, probably as only weeks earlier Thomas had told them he had relinquished all thoughts of marrying Mary. After the wedding, however, he could do nothing other than admit that he had changed his mind. By all accounts, Thomas appears to have been something of a naive and weak-minded character. In view of his family's status – as Gentlemen with considerable power and influence extending far beyond Maiden Newton, the Channings were certainly a cut above the Brookes family and certainly they would not have moved in the same social circles – it would seem that his agreement to the hastily arranged marriage, so far beneath his station, smacked of his bending to persistent persuasion, despite the inevitable disapproval such a match would attract from his family. Under different circumstances, the Channings, after bestowing their consensual blessing on a more agreeable bride, would have

happily arranged a big wedding and celebration for their son at Maiden
Newton. Understandably, when Thomas' parents did find out, they were
extremely upset with the choice that he had made, not to say embarrassed
that the marriage had been kept from them, the *Serious Admonitions to Youth*
finding it 'impossible to express the Grief that their first News of it occa-
sioned'. As far as Thomas' father was concerned he 'could not receive it
without Tears', while his mother, 'whose Darling he was, gave herself over
wholly to an excess of Sorrow, both foreseeing the dismal Consequences
of such a match'. Luckily for Thomas, though, and his imprudent choice
of bride, intervention on the part of some well-meaning relatives restored
'Paternal Affection' and Richard and Elizabeth Channing resolved to stand
by their son and his new wife, expressing a willingness to meet their daughter-in-law and to 'take some Care of their Welfare'. In the circumstances,
this kindness of heart shown by Mary's in-laws was all the more meaningful,
as now that his daughter was off his hands, Richard Brookes wanted nothing
more to with her, bestowing on the couple nothing more than his blessing.

As their life together began, Mary's indifference toward Thomas continued and 'So little was she pleas'd with her Husband's Company' that
she even refused to join him when he returned to run his grocery business
in the town, though her friends eventually persuaded her to take up her
rightful place as dutiful wife – for appearances' sake at least. Moving in a
different sphere now as Mrs Channing, Mary met the friends and business
acquaintances of Thomas who treated her, for the sake of her husband, with
great respect, were being even solicitous enough to pay regular visits on
Mary 'to wean her, if possible, from the loose Company she had been accus-
tom'd to' and presenting 'many Arguments to persuade her into a Love of
her Husband Business'; even if she could not be persuaded to love the man
himself. Presumably, these well-meaning people were also keen to keep a
check on Mary and her activities, in view of her prior reputation. Inevitably,
the disgruntled new wife grew weary of this unaccustomed and unlooked
for company, which she must have found as restrictive as the lifestyle which
was now imposed upon her; we can imagine her nothing but disinterested
and resentful with the situation in which she now found herself – she was
certainly not cut out to be the wife of a grocer. Nevertheless, life went on.

It is a fair assumption that Thomas Channing was grateful to his father
for setting him up in trade and was dedicated to making the grocery business
a success; he was certainly well placed to do so. During the early eighteenth
century, imported foodstuffs came to play a central role in everyday life and
consumption. From the evidence given at Mary's trial we know that raisins

and sugar were sold in the shop, purchased by the 'better off' people in the town. There would have been a good profit margin on these, as on the specialities of tea, coffee and chocolate (sold in cakes which had to be boiled with milk or water), along with other 'exotic' consumables such as spices, tobacco and snuff. Channing's Grocers would have retailed all the usual grocery staples on offer too – and in ranges priced for the discerning gentry's table to goods within the reach of poorer customers, from luxury to utility.

It would not have been untypical for some retailers at this time to simply pile up goods for sale in a room, possibly in a space where the family also lived and slept. The plate glass for windows that would revolutionise shop displays would not become commonplace until the late nineteenth century, when the advent of manufacturing processes made such glazing more financially accessible. Therefore, the enticement of customers was then reliant on perhaps a few oranges or a stick of black sugar (liquorice) displayed in the domestic window indicating that a grocery shop was kept there. While we can only guess as to the look and layout of Channing's Grocers, we can assume that Mr Channing senior had set his son up in premises dedicated to the business, as again we know from evidence given at Mary's trial that the shop premises in Dorchester had a cellar, a lavatory and kitchen attached, with enough additional domestic accommodation for at least one servant. As to where the shop was located in the town, while there is no exact record of the address, in the *Serious Admonitions to Youth* we are told that en route to Mary's execution she was 'dragged' – that is taken in a cart – past her father's and her husband's houses. As shown by Mary's brother's Will, mentioned in the previous chapter, we know that the Brookes family home was located on the north side of High East Street. According to *The Times* newspaper article penned by Thomas Hardy which is covered in detail in Chapter 7, Channing's Grocers occupied the same street. Perhaps the shop was close to old Dorchester's commercial centre, which occupied the area of South Street known as Cornhill, since medieval times the original site of Dorchester's market. The site of the old market house, at the head of the street, is now marked by a limestone obelisk erected in 1784 and formerly the site of the Town Pump. In an area of competitive neighbouring retailers, doubtless Thomas would have invested in the appearance and functionality of his commercial space – a step up from the piles of goods described earlier. From this time on, it became common for grocers to fit out their shops with a counter, shelves and drawers, though of course the visual appeal of the goods would have been impaired on gloomy short winter days; the introduction of gas lighting still being a very long way off, a tallow candle sputtering on the counter would have sufficed. However, such interior fittings allowed for the separation and storage of products, as well as affording the opportunity of a display space, the creative presentation of sugar loaves and boxes and baskets of items helping to sell goods that would have been less eye catching before the advent of branded packaging, as this was a commercial innovation which, like picture windows, would not make an appearance until later in the nineteenth century.

Of course, these considerations were neither here nor there to Mary, who began to make excuses, and fabricate pretexts to be away from the shop as often as possible, as even in the earliest days of her marriage she had taken up again with her former lover. Whether or not Thomas suspected his wife's infidelity, though her trysts were frequent, prudently the lovers never appeared in public together. It was at one of these private assignations that Mary presented the object of her affection with a gold watch as a token of her love – the purchase of which was doubtless funded by the profits of Channing's grocery shop. In the seventeenth century, the style and fashion of watches had changed and men began to wear watches in their pockets instead of as pendants, a fashionable consequence of King Charles II's introduction of the waistcoat in 1675. Even so, until the second half of the eighteenth century, watches remained luxury items; as an indication of how highly they were valued, English newspapers of the eighteenth century often included advertisements offering rewards of between one and five guineas merely for information that might lead to the recovery of a stolen watch. The outlay for a gold watch would have been considerable and while Thomas Channing could not have been blind to his wife's demeanour, not to mention her frequent absences, if he was an astute businessman he may even have begun to notice a discrepancy in his profit margin. Drawing on the old aphorism, that the leopard cannot change his, or her, spots, in an effort then to salvage their short marriage and halt Mary's slide back into her former life, Thomas thought an absence from the scene of so many previous dalliances might remedy the situation. To achieve this, a visit to his parents was judiciously arranged, who, after all, had yet to meet their daughter-in law.

In spite of their earlier misgivings – and probably hoping to make the best of a bad lot – Richard and Elizabeth Channing gave their son's new wife 'a very hearty Welcome' and treated his bride with the utmost civility. Howeve,r the strain told on Mary, 'forced to appear more reserv'd than usual' in the Channings' company and deprived of her 'accustome'd liberty of Discourse or Action,' she availed herself of the opportunity to visit one of Thomas' uncles, in whose company, though she was still subject to a measure of restraint, she nevertheless felt more latitude to be herself. In these less confining surroundings, however, her stay extended to several weeks, during which time Thomas, of necessity, returned to Dorchester to continue running the grocery business. However, after tiring of her company and conversation, Mary showing no inclination to return to her husband, she was finally persuaded to return to Dorchester, the Channing uncle relieved to be rid of his unwelcome house-guest, presumably pleased to be spared the frivolous chatter of a high-spirited 18-year-old.

It was no surprise when, after her return to Dorchester, Mary slipped easily back into her old ways. When Thomas was not preoccupied with diligently keeping shop, he was often absent collecting weekly supplies from the Channing family owned farm at Maiden Newton, the Dorchester shop providing an outlet for some of its produce; this provided Mary ample opportunity to enjoy her social connections and, indeed, to commit adultery. Though Mary had engineered some latitude to enjoy her former life, she was still not entirely unimpeded; at this point, one has to question whether or not she had it in mind to shatter another of the Commandments along with her marriage vows: 'Thou shalt not murder.'

Chapter 3

'This Extravagant course of Life'

As time went by, seemingly unfettered by her married state, Mary increasingly fell back into 'her old course of Living' and threw herself headlong back into the society she had formerly enjoyed before marriage. Frequently entertained at public houses about the town, this was unequivocally unseemly behaviour for a married woman. While Thomas must have felt humiliated, even if he were unaware that he was being cuckolded, he seemed powerless to exercise any husbandly control of his headstrong wife. Indeed, it was legal for a husband to physically chastise an unruly wife, to beat her with a stick for various 'offences' such as lack of obedience to him, provided that the rod was no thicker than his thumb. He was allowed to hit her three times, anywhere on the body, excepting on the head. Clearly, Thomas never had recourse to such 'domestic chastisement' of Mary, though he would have been viewed as well within his rights if he had chosen to do so. The law also permitted a husband to restrain a wife of her liberty, in cases of any gross misbehaviour, which included the refusal of conjugal rights, though this would seem a moot point in view of the fact that Mary had refused to sleep with Thomas from the off. Occasionally, however, the tables were turned, though reported instances of battered husbands are rarely reported; attributable to the humiliation factor, there was the added stigma that a victimized husband would generally be subjected to public derision, because they were perceived as tolerating the abuse they received from their wife.

Incredibly, Thomas also seemed apparently ignorant of many of the 'Treats at Home' that his wife managed to conceal from him, supposedly in the same vein as those seemingly 'innocent' entertainments Mary had hosted in her parent's home, to which her mother was oblivious. Mary was careful enough to hold these gatherings, at which she served costly wines and other fare, on Sundays when her husband's absence was guaranteed while he attended church, or on other opportune days when Thomas was away from home on business, invariably visiting the Channing family-owned farm to collect supplies for the shop. But to gain her full measure of enjoyment, get-togethers were also hosted by neighbours who were happy to 'admit of Treats at their Houses' with Mary still footing the entire bill.

It was apparent, though, even to those amongst her circle of merry friends, that Mary was beginning to overstep the mark. Keeping herself 'under so little Government', her gauche behaviour began to alienate even those of her hardcore partying crowd; exceeding 'the bounds of Modesty' (never one of Mary's strongest attributes) at several of these private entertainments 'her Discourse was so Lewd, and her Actions so indecent' that she even managed to shock some of the male contingent who reproved her for such licentiousness.

Mary's extravagances, which in addition to the expenses she ran up in entertaining also extended to her attire, were also open to public scrutiny, even if Thomas Channing apparently remained blind. Beside the clothes on her back – and we can imagine her spending freely on her husband's credit at the haberdashery and draper's shop on laces and ribbons, silks, brocades and damasks – she would doubtless have purchased other luxury items in the town. Needless to say, Dorchester's gossip-mill ground loudly, to the extent that word of Mary's conduct reached the ear of Thomas' father who, once aware of his daughter-in-law's prodigious outlay, was soon convinced that through her lavish excesses, his son was well on the way to being financially ruined, not to mention his reputation in the town and the stigma that would be attached to the name of Channing family at large. In an indirect attempt to curb Mary's spending and his son's consequent descent into debt, Thomas' father took the drastic step of cutting off his son's credit from London. Mr Channing senior was even willing to take the couple into the family home and provide for them, in a limited manner, in order to prevent Mary's continued and rapid diminishment of the shop's profits. With Thomas now no longer able to purchase any fresh goods with which to replenish the shop-held stock, the income from which was diminishing daily thanks to Mary's constant expenditure, she having scant regard for the business, Thomas now began to have thoughts of leaving her 'to take up another course of Life' rather than face imminent ruin and destitution. The ignominy of either being thrown into prison for unpaid debts, then held until such time as the monies owed were repaid, or even being reduced to dependence on 'poor relief', a parochial welfare system administered by the parish and the pre-cursor to the workhouse, was shameful indeed. The recipients of poor relief were known to be 'on the parish', the shame of pauperisation having received its ultimate symbolic representation in the badging of the poor under the statute of 1697. The act ordered that all poor persons receiving parish relief must wear a badge in red or blue cloth on the shoulder of the right sleeve in an open and visible manner. Presumably, if

Thomas's finances had reached rock bottom, the Channing family would have stepped in and he would have been spared the mortification of reliance upon charity, though whether their financial assistance would have extended to his wife is doubtful. Of course, this became something of a moot point in view of Thomas' death before the eventuality arose.

Several well-meaning friends made attempts to point out to Mary that the 'decay of Trade' in her husband's business had not gone unnoticed in and around town and that she herself was entirely to blame for spending the large sums of money which had resulted in the contracting of great debts 'which would in the end hasten her ruin'; adopting a more thrifty life-style was the only recourse to remedying the Channing's parlous financial circumstances. Yet Mary's callous retort was that their near-ruined situation was entirely the fault of 'her Husband's not understanding his trade'. Another body-blow for Thomas, who, after only twelve weeks of marriage, was facing being reduced to near penury.

Clearly, Mary still had recourse to some lines of credit however, as, the following week being Easter, (Easter Sunday that year fell on 8 April) she was able to provide a 'plentiful and costly entertainment' for a house guest who came to stay with the Channings – a Mr Naile (variously spelt Nail or Nayle) who was an old schoolfellow of Thomas. Though Mary had confined herself – and presumably her budget – earlier in Easter week to 'innocent Mirth' appropriate to the sobriety of the season, after Mr Naile's arrival on the Wednesday or Thursday, the remainder of Easter was spent in 'wonted Excess'. Though those frivolous Easter excesses were an expense that the Channings could ill-afford, perhaps the entire blame should not be squared with Mary. Though her penchant for spending was obvious, it may have been Thomas himself who encouraged this particular outlay, not wanting to highlight the embarrassment of their financial situation to an old friend. Mary got on well with her husband's old school chum, Mr Naile having supposedly paid some previous 'addresses' to Mary when she was single, and she expressed a more than ordinary kindness toward him and a delight in his company – certainly more than she ever thought of showing toward Thomas – so much so, that she prevailed on her husband to give up their own bed, out of hospitality, for their guest's use for the duration of his stay. Bending to his wife's insistence, Thomas was forced to temporarily lodge at a neighbour's house while, on the face of it and in keeping with the seemliness of her married state, Mary said she would take their maid's bed. It seems unlikely that Mary would condescend to allow the maid to share with her so presumably their servant bedded down on the floor, as a generous supposition! As Thomas was seen to be lodging at another house and with the deleterious state of their short marriage presumably common knowledge, naturally this state of domestic affairs 'occasion'd Persons to increase their Censures' – what further insinuations and assumptions would have been drawn had the tattletales known that Mrs Channing was pregnant?

Whether at this time Mary herself knew that she was expecting we do not know. Working backwards from the birth date of her son, born in Dorchester gaol on 19 December 1705, today we can make a reliable reverse calculation as to the date of the baby's conception, tentatively to the last few days in March of that year. While of course the date of Thomas and Mary's wedding meant that it was entirely feasible that the child was his, after the debacle of the failed wedding night bedding ritual, it is entirely probable that the marriage was never in fact consummated, given Mary's repugnance toward her husband and the unseemly haste with which she took back her former lover. While her married status provided the perfect legitimacy for her condition, if the marriage had indeed remained unconsummated then, of course, Thomas Channing would sooner or later have been aware that the child was not his. All this calls into question the timing and the motive behind Mary's next drastic move, which was to be her ultimate undoing.

If these were indeed the circumstances in which Mary found herself, one might wonder whether or not she had considered availing herself of any of the contraceptive choices which would have been available to her at the time, though even if she had, these were mostly ineffective. The popularity of condoms was limited, made of either animal intestines or linen soaked in vinegar; this method of birth control was also linked to vice and was mostly practiced in houses of ill repute. Pessaries and douches would also have been available, as well as any number of herbal concoctions, obtainable from the 'cunning folk' alluded to in the first chapter, who could also assist with the preparation of a herbal abortifacient if other measures had failed. The centuries old concoctions of Pennyroyal and Tansy were well known, though Tansy (*tanacetum vulgare*), also called bitter buttons, was thought to aid conception as well as induce abortions. Either way, there was a high risk of endangering the life of the mother, not to mention the legal ramifications – at the time, procuring or performing an abortion was against the law. Prior to 1803, abortion or the offence of 'attempting to induce a miscarriage' was punishable by a fine or short term of imprisonment, though of course the shameful cost in the irretrievable loss of one's good character would have been immeasurable. The only other desperate alternative, that of infanticide, was a crime which carried the death penalty, though a woman could be found guilty, under a statute passed in 1624, even if she simply tried to hide her pregnancy and later miscarried, or if the infant was stillborn.

Nevertheless, the fact remained that Mary was expecting and, allowing some latitude either side of the supposed conception date, it is feasible that Mary was aware of her condition in the early stages. Indeed, the conception date may have been earlier – while, anecdotally, firstborns are often said to be late, contemporary studies into this old wives' tale have shown that only a slight percentage of first babies are often carried past their term and, in turn, the rigours of Mary's later imprisonment may also have induced an earlier confinement. Regardless of whether Mary was aware of the pregnancy, or doubted the paternity of the child she was carrying, as Thomas was the primary impediment to the hedonistic lifestyle that she strove to enjoy, she may simply have desired to be rid of her husband, regardless of her dubious enceinte state.

Whether her strategy had been long in the planning, (though the marriage was only thirteen weeks old) or a spur of the moment idea, possibly prompted by the realisation of the irrefutable proof of her infidelity, at about 4 o'clock the following Monday afternoon, 16 April – she had possibly awaiting the departure of their houseguest – Mary purchased some poison from a neighbouring apothecary's shop.

Since Medieval times, the increase in the establishment of apothecary shops in many towns and cities meant that any number of toxic substances were easily available for purchase. As the range of substances on offer was intended for either medicinal use or often employed in domestic pest control, namely arsenic and mercury, the purchase of these unrestricted substances usually went unquestioned, though of course they could be employed for more malign purposes. After all, as Alfred Swaine Taylor the nineteenth century toxicologist is quoted as saying, 'A poison in a small dose is a medicine, a medicine in a large dose is a poison.'

With regards to arsenic, for example, which as we shall see was Mary's initial poison of choice, because of the number of murder cases involving the poison, in 1851 the government was eventually forced to introduce the 'Arsenic Act' forbidding the sale of any arsenic compounds to a purchaser who was unknown to the supplying pharmacist. Would-be poisoners were further thwarted by the introduction of a requirement that all manufacturers of arsenic powder should mix one ounce of a colouring agent (indigo or soot were usually employed) to every pound of arsenic powder produced, though this was all cold comfort to those earlier victims who had already succumbed to the hand of the poisoner.

Before the development in Taylor's time of analytical chemistry increasing the risk that a poisoner would be caught – and indeed, the measures put in place to hinder the arsenic poisoner – poison was popularly seen as a method of murder frequently employed by females. Requiring no physical exertion, the lady of the house was also ideally placed to conveniently administer a poison as they were predominantly involved with the preparation of food and the management of and access to household remedies and 'medicines'; this was a circumstance which Mary took good advantage of. Though many poisoners disguised their murderous intent beneath the misdirected belief that the doses they administered were in fact 'remedies', Mary indulged in no such stratagem and went straight in for the kill.

On the Monday afternoon in question, Mary had called at Mr Wolmington's Apothecary shop and asked the assistant for some 'ratsbane'. As the name would suggests, a white powdered poisonous trioxide of arsenic, ratsbane was commonly used as a pesticide and was, as a by-product of the emerging smelting industry, cheap and readily available. Though it later became the poison of choice in Victorian melodrama and the popular press, a significant proportion of the fatalities caused by arsenic were more pedestrian, resulting from accidental use in food. Arsenic is virtually odourless and tasteless and easily confused with flour or sugar and other cooking essentials; doubtless Mary was aware of this fact and this was why she had asked for it. In later attempts to prevent deaths through unintentional ingestion and misidentification, poison bottles were given distinctive features; coloured glass bottles like cobalt blue, inky black, and dark green ensured they were easily recognizable, as well as having raised lettering or inlays of the words on the glass, especially useful if you were fumbling by candlelight. Patterns included latticework, deep grooves, geometric shapes and, most commonly, the skull and crossbones, which would have been particularly useful in instances where the original label had peeled off or if the consumer was illiterate. However, these precautionary manufacturing measures would not appear in England until the 1750s, so all of this was of no use to poor Thomas or unwanted spouses of the time.

Despite her best laid plans, Mary was thwarted in her purchase of arsenic, however, as there was no ratsbane available in Mr Wolmington's shop that day; but she was offered mercury by the shop assistant instead. While for centuries mercury was an essential part of many different medicines, such as diuretics, antibacterial agents, antiseptics, laxatives and not least in the treatment of syphilis, the sexually transmitted disease which had long been the scourge of Europe, the mercury-based remedies that the sick and ailing endured were hardly efficacious and many patients died of mercury poisoning. Mercury toxicity most commonly affects the neurologic, gastro-intestinal and renal systems and can happen both accidentally and deliber-ately by exposure to water-soluble forms of the element, such as mercuric chloride, a white crystalline solid, archaically known as 'corrosive subli-mate'. It must have been this form of 'salts of white mercury' that Mary purchased. Though she had offered Mary mercury as an in-stock alternative to ratsbane, initially the shop assistant said that she could not find the right container, so she would have to wait for her master to return. Clearly set on her course, Mary took it upon herself to look and, finding what she wanted, 'took a piece about the bigness of a Walnut' and paying a farthing for it — that is, one quarter of an old penny with a relative worth today of about 15 pence, certainly an inexpensive if lethal commodity — secreted the purchase in her bosom and left the shop. This not as bizarre as it may sound, because, before the advent of the hand-bag, women would keep valuables in either pear-shaped pockets, tied around the waist usually underneath their skirts and accessed through openings in the side seams of their petticoats, or in the absence of pockets, small items could be tucked safely into their bodice. However discreetly Mary concealed her purchase, there were nevertheless a number of witnesses in Mr Wolmington's shop on that April afternoon, whose testimony will be related later and of course, Amy Clavel, the apothe-cary shop assistant, was one of them.

The following day, on the Tuesday morning, Mary asked their maid, Elizabeth Cosins, who was working in the Channing's grocers shop at the time, to call her master up from the cellar as his breakfast was ready and waiting on the kitchen table. Mary had prepared a dish of boiled milk with rice, a common enough breakfast dish as by the beginning of the eighteenth century the import of rice had become common and rice pudding was some-thing of an everyday staple, being served at any time of the day. Thomas duly made his way to the kitchen as bidden by his wife and although their maid had returned to keep shop, she could still overhear her master and mistress's conversation: Thomas complained about the taste of his break-fast, that it was nauseous and that he could 'eat but a few Spoonfuls'. In her later testimony, and under oath, the Channing's maid stated that Thomas had said his 'Milk was gristy', most probably a description of the texture; the word's exact meaning is unclear today, as the word has fallen into disuse. Undaunted, Mary tried to persuade Thomas to try his breakfast again, but on his refusal to eat any more, Mary took the food from him, saying 'this is gristy indeed' and proceeded to throw the remainder into the 'House of

Office' – a common name for the lavatory in seventeenth century England – and washed the dish herself, thus eliminating any evidence of the poison. Though Thomas had only managed to eat a small amount of his breakfast, Mary had 'so well seasoned it' that her husband immediately felt 'very unwell' and within half an hour began vomiting. Though Thomas in no way suspected that his wife had attempted to poison him, what happened next, in itself rather stomach turning, persuaded some of the Channing's neighbours to believe that some foul play was to blame for his sudden state of ill-health; a dog which had happened to lick up some of the breakfast that Thomas had so violently expelled 'was taken with the same Distemper'.

Suspicions aroused, a physician was sent for. On his arrival, agreeing with the general consensus that poison was to blame, 'a speedy Application of proper Remedies' was administered – namely a gastric lavage, more commonly known as a stomach pump of oil and water to cleanse the patient's stomach. Though these rudimentary emetics had some beneficial effect, Thomas Channing appearing 'something better', by the following day, Wednesday, the symptoms were still persisting and, with the increase of 'tormenting pains', it was later presumed that Mary had administered a further dose of poison; tellingly, she had remained by her husband's bedside throughout. In John Hutchins' *The History and Antiquities of the County of Dorset*, the author states in a footnote concerning Mary's case that she had 'poisoned him by giving him white mercury, first in rice milk, and twice afterwards in a glass of wine', while in the 1914 publication of *Highways and Byways in Dorset*, Sir Frederick Treves borrows this assertion, but in reduced measure: 'At last she poisoned him, they said, by giving him white mercury, first in rice milk and then in a glass of wine'. At this point, Thomas Channing himself may even have begun to suspect his wife, as that day he hastily wrote his will and as can be seen from the transcription below, bequeathed his entire estate to his father except for the 'one shilling' that he left to his wife, 'having every good reason to give her no more'.

Last Will & Testament of Thomas Channing

*This is the last Will and Testament of me Thomas-
CHANING of Dorchester in the County of Dorset Grocer
Made this that eighteenth day of April in the
year of our Lord Christ according to the computation of the
Church of England One Thousand Seven Hundred and
Five I give all my estate real and personal unto my*

dear father Richard CHANING gent saving only one
shilling I give my wife having every good reason to give
her no more. I make my said father my full and whole
executor of this my Will and Testament in witness
whereof I have hereunto set my hand and seal the day and
year above written

Signed Tho: CHANING

Sealed, published and declared to
be the last will and Testament of the
said Thomas CHANING in the
presence of
Elizabeth WADMAN and Thomas COOPER

Probate granted May 21st 1705

Bequeathing one shilling to a beneficiary in a will was fairly common practice at this date and was used where a person who might normally be expected to inherit was to be excluded – it was a simple and effective way of demonstrating they had been considered, preventing them from contesting the Will later. This type of bequest, therefore, normally had no overt connotations, yet, given the specific wording, this was clearly not the case in this instance.

Needless to say, word of the drama playing out at the Channing's house, the doctor being called in, the speedy decline in Thomas' condition and the supposed cause of his ailment soon reached the streets of Dorchester. As folk began to talk, it reached Mary's ear that she was known to have purchased poison from the apothecary's shop that Monday, gossip which was presumably put about by any of the number of the witnesses later called at her trial who had been in the shop when she had asked to buy poison. Fearing exposure, Mary, in an uncharacteristically submissive manner, 'earnestly entreated Mr. Wolmington the Apothecary not to do her a Diskindness' and begged him to make no mention of the fact that she had purchased mercury from his shop. Whether Mr Wolmington initially obliged, he certainly gave damning evidence later in court.

In the meantime, news of Thomas' condition had travelled as far as Maiden Newton and his concerned father arrived in Dorchester on Thursday, with hopes that he might find his son's health improved – though perhaps he too had his suspicions as he immediately forced Mary from the sick room. Though his son was of a weak-willed and easily manipulated nature, Richard Channing was certainly made of sterner stuff and in the face of his anger at finding his son in such a parlous state of health, understandably Mary gathered together the best of her clothes and other items of value and fled the marital home that same afternoon. She was bold enough however to mask her indecently hasty departure by confidently walking through the streets of Dorchester, even laughing at the jeers of several children who on seeing her threatened her with the stake – an allusion to the mode of execution for those wives found guilty of murdering their husband. A prophetic jibe indeed.

Though Mary was now gone, Thomas continued to linger on in agony. Even if the attending doctor's remedy had been of any effect, no amount of purging his patient would prevent the inevitable, besides which, having found the poison 'had seized his lungs', Thomas Channing's nearest and dearest were told to prepare for the worst. By Saturday evening, the doctor noted that 'his pulse was quite gone' and at about nine o'clock, 'with a hisking Cough, like a rotten sheep' Thomas Channing died.

Though the intimation of the one shilling bequest made to Mary in Thomas Channing's will would seem to confirm his suspecting his wife of making an attempt on his life, the request that Thomas made on the Friday afternoon before he expired is therefore all the more surprising, and indeed formed the inspirational basis for Thomas Hardy's ballad, *The Mock Wife*, the title alluding to the now folkloric tale of what was supposedly done to satisfy the dying wish of Thomas Channing; the poetical insights of which will be explored in a later chapter. Whether fact or fiction, the account given in the *Serious Admonitions to Youth* bear repetition here:

> 'The afternoon before he [Thomas Channing] died he gave a particular Instance of his Love and Charity for his Wife, tho' sensible that she was the occasion of his Death. Two young Women coming to see him, the Nurse asked him if he would not speak to his Wife, whom she had prevail'd with one of them to [im]personate, and she being brought pretty near, with great eagerness, he rose up and kissed her, and (being desired to do it) freely forgave her.'

Perhaps faced with the prospect of meeting his Maker, Thomas was inclined to forgiveness on his deathbed, in order to gain for himself a measure of closure and inner peace. But this must have been cold comfort for his parents. His disconsolate mother, 'whose Tears were scarce dried up for the Grief, occassion'd by his first Step to Destruction', that being her son's marriage to Mary, was 'now quite overwhelmed with Sorrow' and we are told that her lamentations were shared by the populace of Dorchester at large, the consternation of the townsfolk 'unexpressible, every Person being seized with Horror at the News of such a Fact.' For his part, Thomas' father, with a clearer head, requested that his son's body be 'opened', that is he asked for an autopsy to be performed in order to satisfy the widespread suspicion of foul play. Accordingly, on the Monday following Thomas' death, a post mortem was carried out; both the doctor and the surgeon officiating expressed the shared opinion that the cause of death had been poisoning and 'that there remain'd not the least ground of doubt'. Though it would be near on five decades, in 1752, before the advancement of anatomical study in England was greatly improved with the passing of an Act that allowed judges to substitute dissection instead of a sentence of hanging in a metal cage at the gibbet after execution, it would nevertheless be wrong to assume that the standards of forensic investigations practised by the medical fraternity at this time were entirely crude, or to suggest that the surgeons and doctors were not competent in their conduct of autopsies. Yet observation was the basis on which informed decisions were made as to the rudimentary cause of death and in the absence of any reliable toxicological testing – coincidentally first used to secure a murder conviction in 1752, the same year that the 'Murder Act' referred to above was introduced – necessarily, the opinions of attending physicians and surgeons was relied upon as conclusive.

Having 'before opened Bodies that had been poisoned' the doctor's findings were indeed accepted as conclusive. He reported finding symptoms of poison throughout Thomas' whole body, particularly in the lungs which were 'almost interily [sic] discoloured'. The bottom of the stomach and part of the liver were also found to be black and the presence of several black spots in the 'guts', that is the intestines, was also noted.

As Thomas was still alive when Mary had fled, so far she was still unaware that her presumed actions had rendered her a widow, as by the time her husband died, she was already in hiding. After her feigned confident departure, though she appeared unconcerned to her friends, Mary was not seen in public again until her arrest. One of her friends had concealed her in a house in Dorchester on the Thursday evening after she had so hastily left, prompted by the ire of Richard Channing; she was also harboured there the Friday night following and in spite of the 'diligent search made by the Officers', her hiding place remained undiscovered. As there was no police constabulary in the modern sense until the Dorset County Constabulary was formed in 1855, pursuant to the right given to boroughs to establish police forces along Metropolitan (London) lines in their own areas, the 'Officers' who were involved in the search for Mary were almost certainly Constables of the Watch under the direction of a magistrate.

Having evaded detection thus far, though obviously fearful of arrest, Mary left the safe house under cover of dark that Friday night, according to the *Serious Admonitions to Youth*, making for a parish about four miles away. It is easy to see how Mary could have arranged her flight, with her father running his own business as a wagoner, she could have hitched a ride to a nearby village with one of his wagon drivers. Yet clearly, she still felt exposed and vulnerable to capture as she spent the best part of Saturday hiding in a neighbouring wood. From this we can suppose that Mary had fled toward Puddletown, a parish indeed some four and a half miles northeast of Dorchester- it was formerly known as used Piddletown, the name being changed for reasons of social decorum! – where Thorncombe Wood, still a part of the Puddletown Forest lying to the south east of the village, would have provided decent cover. Though the route would have traversed the dark heath on the western edge of the forest, with its stretch of old Roman Road which could be threatening to the lonely traveller, bolstered by tales of a phantom Roman centurion haunting the ancient route to Dorchester from Badbury Rings, Mary urgently needed to conceal herself. Clearly, she could not remain hidden in the wood for long as she had already been spotted in the vicinity, possibly as a consequence of the search arranged for Mary by her father-in-law. After the enquiries in Dorchester had turned up nothing, Richard Channing saw to it that 'Hue and Cries were immediately sent into all Parts' and notice of Mary's flight posted in all the main surrounding towns and villages, with 'a great many imploy'd [sic] all that night in searching the Wood where she had been seen that Day.' With Mary's pursuers hot on her heels, those amongst her loyal friends took it upon themselves to employ a trustworthy person to convey Mary that evening to Charlton Wortborn in Somerset where she had family – in all likelihood, the village of Charlton Horethorne, about four miles north of Sherborne, close to the Dorset and Somerset border. There, she was lodged with a relation of her brother's wife and as nobody in her sister-in-law's household was yet aware of the events that had taken place in Dorchester, for a while, at least, Mary felt safe.

After the sighting of Mary in the wood, several people in Dorchester were committed and questioned on suspicion of having assisted in her escape and, while no useful information was forthcoming, the man who had escorted Mary into Somerset must have been rattled as, on Sunday, no doubt alarmed at the damning prospect of being named an accessory, not to mention also possibly being persuaded by the reward offered by Richard Channing, the 'trustworthy' person in the pay of her friends gave up her location over the county line; as a further measure of his contrition he also offered to bring Mary back to Dorchester to face her accusers.

That same day, accompanied by two others, Mary's turn-coat accomplice returned to Charlton and managed to persuade her to return with him to Dorchester, employing the ruse that her husband had in fact recovered and wished to speak with her. Mary must have indeed been surprised, if not somewhat relieved, to learn that Thomas had not succumbed to her efforts to poison him – even if she failed to rue her actions, at least she would no longer be facing a murder charge. First conveyed to Sherborne, it was here however that Mary first learned that Thomas was in fact dead. On the news being broken to her, Mary nevertheless showed 'little or no Concern'. After spending the night at Sherborne, presumably under close watch, on Monday morning Mary was taken back to Dorchester, around a thirty mile journey, to be examined by the authorities for her part in the untimely death of Thomas Channing. Whether she was conveyed in a coach, open wagon or closely led on horseback, the journey would have taken the best part of the day and it may well have been dusk by the time Mary arrived back in Dorchester, though she may have wished that night had already fallen if she were to avoid the derisive looks and comments of the townsfolk who doubtless had already judged her guilty of murder.

Chapter 4

'That Perfection in Wickedness...'

After the arrest party had returned to Dorchester – we can imagine Richard Channing's desire for justice was at least partially sated by his daughter-in-law's apprehension – in all likelihood Mary would have been held under house-arrest rather than being committed to the town gaol prior to her being questioned the following day. In accordance with the eighteenth century criminal justice system, Richard Channing would have initiated Mary's prosecution by bringing a criminal complaint against her before Dorchester's Justices of the Peace. Once a criminal complaint was brought before him, a Justice of the Peace had a number of options, depending on the nature of the complaint, the wishes of the complainant, and his own preferences. Mary was examined at a pre-trial hearing; at such hearings the evidence against accused criminals was assembled and vetted, in Mary's case by the Mayor, John Nelson, re-elected for a second term in 1704, as well as various other Justices of the Peace. On being questioned, Mary responded with an emphatic declaration of her innocence; to back up her avowal, she voluntarily offered to clear herself by going to see and touch her husband's dead body.

Though on the face of it this might seem a strange defence on Mary's part, since ancient times many European courts relied on a type of trial by ordeal that involved a 'bleeding' corpse, an ancient method of ascertaining the guilt or innocence of accused murderers. The 'bier-right', or *cruentation*, was based on the belief that the body is still able to hear and act a short time after death, so that if a murderer approached or touched the corpse of their victim, then the corpse would bleed or froth at the mouth. While England stopped using the bier-right at the end of the seventeenth century, the method was one that remained in the collective consciousness and Mary was obviously well aware of the credence once placed on the practice. Whether she herself believed in it, she must have thought it would support her case, though 'purge fluid' or decomposition fluid which drains from the mouth, nose and other orifices during putrefaction, looking a lot like blood, must have been the grounding for many mistaken accusations of murder.

While initially Mayor Nelson and the assembled Justices agreed to grant Mary's request, 'upon more mature Consideration' they had a change of heart and the prisoner was immediately recalled. At this point, as Mary refused to answer any further questions put to her, she was committed to the town gaol.

However, Mary was not remanded within the walls of the Dorchester's present prison, as this building was not completed until 1795 – though now closed, HM Prison Dorchester is still something of an iconic edifice in the town, occupying the site of a previous twelfth century Norman castle. It was outside this prison that the 16-year-old Thomas Hardy witnessed the hanging of Elizabeth Martha Brown, the last woman to be publicly hanged in Dorset, executed on gallows erected over the prison gates in 1856 and held to be the inspiration for Hardy's ill-fated heroine in *Tess of the D'Urbervilles*. This and other of Hardy's Dorchester inspirations will be discussed in a later chapter.

The former HM Prison Dorchester was in fact the last of the town's gaols, closed amidst much controversy in 2013 and destined for conversion into private housing. Nevertheless, there has been a county gaol in Dorchester since the medieval period, a charter granted in the reign of Edward I in 1305 giving Dorchester the right to operate the county gaol, which effectively confirmed its status as county town. In his *The History of Dorchester* James Savage wrote in 1837 that 'The county gaol stood anciently where the public house called the Angel was situated.' But the capacity of the original gaol obviously proved inadequate as in 1623, the lack of a common gaol for the County was recognised and the High Sheriff, the Justices of the Peace and others purchased land in (High) East street in Dorchester and spent at least £1,000 in erecting one which was completed in the summer of 1624, intended to accommodate among others 'incorrigible rogues', mainly those prosecuted as vagabonds. Sited on the corner of Icen Way and High East Street, the northern intersecting end of Icen Way was once aptly called Gaol Lane, and it was in this gaol that Mary was committed.

Though prison conditions at the beginning of the eighteenth century were grim to say the least – the old Dorchester gaol was sold off in 1793 after the renowned prison architect William Blackburn condemned the facilities as inadequate – with inmates denied the solitude to reflect on their crimes as well as no ventilation and access to open spaces. Initially, while she awaited trial, Mary's confinement was not so onerous. Thanks to their affluence, her parents were able to pay for respectable accommodation for their daughter as prisoners on remand awaiting their trial were required to pay the gaoler for their board and lodging and, as in all things, money talks. Yet later, when their support payments lapsed, Mary was exposed to a more spartan confinement, as the conditions in Dorchester gaol were like any other prison at the time, with prisoners without means massed together in damp, insanitary and overcrowded conditions. It was in this gaol, some years prior to Mary's incarceration, that a number of the prisoners held in the aftermath of the Monmouth rebellion died, succumbing to the squalid conditions which bred 'gaol fever'. There was no privacy, segregation of the sexes nor protection from other inmates, with all kinds of prisoners held together – men, women, children, the insane, serious recidivists and petty criminals, as well as those awaiting trial and those actually serving a term of imprisonment as their sentence. In addition, some prisoners were those being held who were unable to meet their debts, by far the largest element in the eighteenth century prison population, often innocent tradespeople who had fallen on hard times and kept in prison until they paid what was owed. This of course was a fate that might have eventually befallen Thomas Channing, had he lived, his creditors taking legal action should Mary have continued to fritter away the profits from the grocery business with her extravagant ways.

In the meantime, though she was in gaol, Mary was dismissive with regard to the gravity of her situation and, unconcerned, continued to live 'but little different from what she had done before, the Circumstances of a Prison considered'. The *Serious Admonitions to Youth* did however note that she refused to be seen, excepting visits made by those of 'her intimate Acquaintance'. Incredibly, in spite of her imprisonment, before long Mary's need for society shone through and she was soon receiving visits from many others and 'affected to appear more gawdy [sic] on such Days' when she expected company, only refusing admittance to her room if she were not suitably attired. Unfettered, so to speak, by her confinement, when visits from the outside were not forthcoming, Mary diverted herself with the company of her fellow prisoners, presumably also awaiting trial, their circumstances allowing a similar liberty of movement within the confines of the gaol, though she would adjust 'her Carriage and Discourse according to the different Temper of her Visitors'. To those who visited out of curiosity at her situation, she would appear pleasant and unconcerned, discoursing with the 'Delight of her past Mirth and Jollity', spending hours with them in the cellar of other 'rooms' in the gaol where there was 'an Opportunity of Drinking'. While Mary may well have been furnished with some 'home comforts' by her parents or other well-wishing friends, alcohol in the form of beer was available to anyone within the gaol, so long as they could pay for it and clearly the sale of beer, along with the supply of other consumables, presented ample opportunity for corruption.

In 1638, as a consequence of a series of abuses on the part of Dorchester's 'Keeper of the Gaol', a series of directives were drawn up for 'orders for the better government of the gaole [sic] and Mainprise (those being held without bail in a county gaol) in Dorchester'. One of these directives stated that the gaoler was not to brew beer himself for the prisoners, but to purchase it in the town, at twelve shillings a hogshead of best beer, which was to be sold at 1d (penny) per quart, while 'small beer' (beer or ale with a very low alcohol content) was to be purchased at six shillings per hogshead, again in the town, then sold to prisoners at 1d for two quarts. Mentioned in another of the same directives, the Keeper was to be allocated the sum of 1d per day per prisoner 'to be allowed to the gaoler for bread to feed the poor prisoners *who are to have their full allowance*' (my italics). In respect of bread for other prisoners, the gaoler was to make no more than 1d profit on every dozen loaves. Clearly, those same men in authority who had ordered the building of the new gaol in 1623 were also on the make, as by order of the sheriff and magistrates, all grain used in the gaol was be ground at the mills that they owned in Fordington and if the gaoler bought in his bread, he should buy it only from bakers who ground their corn at those mills. The opportunities for capitalising on the supply and demand of the prison population further extended to accommodation costs, the same orders stating that 'the maximum rent to be charged to prisoners for their rooms in the gaol is to be 14d per week, and only 6d per week in the Rendezvous chamber' – a room set aside for conjugal visits – and again open to exploitation.

The opportunity for corruption was of course commonplace throughout the entire prison system and in no way specific to Dorchester – clearly not all criminals were behind bars! In 1706, the same year that Mary was executed, the Keeper of York Castle Gaol was 'Turnkey' Thomas Ward, noted for his corruption and the exploitation of his position, charging a fee for showing visitors round the cells. He was a bully and an extortionist and forced prisoners to buy food and drink from him at inflated prices. In York, matters came to a head in 1709 when prisoners signed a petition against the Turnkey's 'inhumane and unchristian' behaviour. Nevertheless, Ward remained in his position and in 1718 rose to become the Governor of York Castle Gaol.

Where female prisoners were concerned, there was yet another opportunity to make money from abuse of the system, as under English common law 'pleading the belly' permitted women in the later stages of pregnancy to be reprieved of their death sentences until after the delivery of the child, a situation pertinent to Mary case, which will necessarily be discussed in more detail later. While the plea did not constitute a defence and could only be made after a guilty verdict had been passed, suffice to say such a successful plea nevertheless extended the life expectancy of the condemned mother to be and in some instances a pardon was secured, so it was clearly a more than worthwhile ploy. Consequently, it was not uncommon for women under sentence of death to enlist the assistance of their gaolers in allowing access to gentlemen for such a purpose, a circumstance alluded to by John Gay in *The Beggar's Opera* (1728), the character Filch making an extra income as a 'child getter ... helping the ladies to a pregnancy against their being called down to sentence'.

Of course, the services of the gaoler himself could be enlisted and as a deterrent, gaolers, Keepers or local sheriffs in charge of any female prisoner who fell pregnant while held in their custody were subject to a fine. In an attempt to limit the abuse of the system further, the law decreed that no woman could be granted a second reprieve on an original sentence passed if she were later found to be with child. Yet the threat of a fine did not always present an effective deterrent, Turnkey Ward being an obvious case in point. A female prisoner named Mary Burgan, in his charge after being convicted of infanticide in 1705, became pregnant while awaiting execution and in all likelihood, Ward was the father. In this instance, Burgan was allowed to live in the prison with her son, tellingly named Thomas, who grew up in York Castle Gaol, supported by payments made by the Three Ridings until 1718 when he was put out to apprenticeship at the age of 12. Mary had been listed as a reprieve in the Calendar of Felons for York Castle 1707, her sentence being subsequently commuted to that of transportation, but it appears that she was eventually released under a general pardon issued by Queen Anne in 1710, the power of pardon being a royal prerogative of mercy in the gift of the monarch of the United Kingdom, most frequently cited in cases where the death penalty had been given. Indeed, the same entreaties would be made on behalf of Mary Channing after her trial, but clemency was not guaranteed, as we shall see.

Returning to Mary's behaviour during her earlier confinement, namely the reception of visitors, she must have been disquieted by the call paid on her by one of Thomas Channing's relations. To this unwelcome visitor, she certainly made her feeling clear 'who she thought had acted too much against her'. Expressing her 'Unconcernedness at all they [the Channing family] could do', she declared that she was confident in her ability to 'frustrate all their Consultations, baffle the Pleadings of the Counsel, and make her Innocence appear to the World'. Even when she was taken to task over her past extravagances, Mary vindicated her behaviour rather than excusing it, asserting that she 'would have increased it, had she known she would have so soon been deprived of the Means to continue it'. Yet, in spite of Mary bravado, descriptions of which were no doubt related back to an incensed Richard Channing, thereby increasing his efforts to thwart her acquittal, perhaps disquieted by the visit from her husband's kinsman, she did appear contrite to those who subsequently saw her and who were intent on convincing Mary of the consequence of her crime, 'to bring her to a Sense of her miserable Condition, and do some Good to her Soul'. In this different temper, in a more serious frame of mind, Mary began to talk of death and 'another World', and though she stoutly maintained her innocence, she 'daily endeavour'd to prepare for Death, and bring herself into a Condition fit for it, in case her Enemies should so far prevail as to take away her Life'.

Though she protested her innocence, Mary obviously harboured concerns over the outcome of her impending trial for the murder of her husband, in all likelihood sensible of the weight that Richard Channing would bring to bear on the proceedings and in her desperation, she engineered an escape plan. As a remand prisoner, Mary's confinement was less than rigorous. Her contrived means of escape was to persuade the under-keeper of the gaol to allow her to go out in the night, ostensibly to visit her mother. Around midnight on the agreed date, forcing the door to her room, which led onto a gallery which in turn led out of the prison (presumably it was at this point that the under-keeper was to 'turn a blind eye') Mary, accompanied by a young woman with whom she shared her room, having made it thus far must have thought they were home free, but on being overheard by some of the other prisoners, with the subsequent commotion their break-out was thwarted; understandably, from that time on Mary was kept under closer scrutiny. One has to wonder whether the under-keeper was disciplined as a consequence. This particular avenue of liberty now firmly blocked, Mary could do no more than await her upcoming trial.

Before her case came before the assizes, however, Mary's parents tried their utmost to prevent a guilty verdict being returned. In a bid to clear their daughter's name, Mary's eldest brother, who was a silversmith, declared that he himself had asked Mary to purchase the poison for his own particular use in his trade. Used in the process of 'fire gilding', mercury ground up with gold to create an amalgam can be applied to the silver surface; after heating in an oven to drive off the mercury as a toxic vapour, the gold was bound to the surface of the work giving a gilded impression, either in that of the design or to give the appearance that the object was actually made of gold. However, Richard Channing, who maintained the statement to be false, was concerned that this 'Stratagem might save her Life' and took immediate legal steps, issuing a Bill of Indictment against Mary's brother – that is, a formal written accusation as presented to a jury that a person has committed a crime – and so prevented his evidence coming to trial. And so the matter proceeded to court.

Depending on the severity of an accusation, prisoners could spend some considerable time on remand awaiting trial before the next Assize Courts. Assizes were periodic courts held around England and Wales, conducted twice yearly in 'rural' circuits, with the judges travelling on horseback, usually in pairs, from county to county to hear cases. Dorset fell under the Western Circuit, which also included Hampshire, Wiltshire, Devonshire, Somersetshire and Cornwall, and each circuit lasted between two and five weeks depending on the number of cases to be heard. At these Assize Courts, capital offences were heard, committed to it by the quarter sessions, the local county courts held four times per year and without the authority to try capital offences. The cases of those accused of capital offences included the crimes of murder, manslaughter and rape as well as treason, major fraud or theft, arson, riot and rebellion. Guilt on any of these counts carried the death penalty before 1836, the year in which capital punishment was abolished for crimes other than those of murder, attempted murder and treason, the last being the crime for which those tried at Dorchester by Judge Jeffreys in 1685 were accused, in the wake of the Monmouth Rebellion.

As Mary had been committed to gaol after the Lent assizes for the Western Circuit had been held, Thomas Channing dying on Saturday, 21 April, a fortnight after Easter, she had to wait for the summer session. These commenced at Winchester, then moved on to hear cases at Salisbury before proceeding onto Dorchester, after which the judges would go to Exeter, then either Bodmin or Truro, finally sitting at either Wells or Bridgewater, and as a rule attending in that order.

The proceedings for Assize courts in Dorchester were held at the Old Crown Court within the Old Shire Hall building. First mentioned in 1638 when enlargements to the building, costing £60, were made, at that time, as the court only sat for a few weeks a year the building was utilised for other purposes, including the storage of gunpowder during the Civil War. The Shire Hall was also a workplace, and in 1650 the poor were paid sixpence a day to beat hemp in the jail room.

In 1705, the Dorchester Summer Assizes began on the Thursday 26 July and lasted three days, until 28 July, the Saturday on which Mary's case was heard, with Mr Justice Price presiding. Robert Price was a politician as well as a judge – he had served as Member of Parliament for Weobley in Herefordshire before resigning the seat in favour of his elder son, Thomas, in 1702, as Queen Anne upon her succession in that year had elevated Price to the bench as a Baron of the Exchequer. An experienced judge, Price's legal career began when he became attorney-general for South Wales in 1682, and he was clearly an advocate of the established church; presiding over one particular case at the Winchester summer assize preceding Dorchester that year, Justice Price was noted as having given an 'extraordinary … charge' to the grand jury 'in which among other things he took notice of the slanders and aspersions which the fanatic party in the libels etc. cast on the Church of England, and reminded them that the present liberty which they enjoyed was purely the effect of the bounty of the Church of England'. After issuing such admonishments at Winchester, Justice Price faced the prospect of further dusty roads before him as he continued on the court circuit to Dorchester - historical meteorological records for 1705 indicate that this was 'a dry year; Mild & Dark' and if Justice Price had been called on to covered the Western Circuit for the preceding Lent Assizes he may well have experienced the fogs and close weather during the first half of March preceding the dry summer in the south that year.

As Mary's trial began, at about 10 o'clock that Saturday morning as the court apparently was late in assembling, we can imagine the stuffy and crowded courtroom. Doubtless, the public gallery was packed with those self-same voracious Dorchester gossips for whom Mary's antics and later more serious misdemeanours had provided fodder, though in some courthouses, access to the public gallery was restricted by the ability to pay. Courthouse officials in the court of King's (or Queen's in this instance) Bench were known to charge for entry. The staff of the Old Bailey had the right to charge fees for admission to the galleries, one way in which the demand for admissions to witness the proceedings of high profile cases was limited.

Though the Old Crown Court in which Mary was tried was replaced by the building now occupying the Old Shire Hall, it is a fair assumption that the old layout conformed to the same basic design of London's Old Bailey at that time. Arranged so as to emphasise the contest between the accused and the rest of the court, Mary would have stood at 'the bar' or 'dock', in those days actually a bar of iron, directly facing the witness box, where

A Catalogue of the severall Sects and Opinions in England and other Nations. With a briefe Rehearsall of their false and dangerous Tenents.

Broadsheet of 1647 - Catalogue of the Severall Sects and Opinions in England and other Nations
Included amongst the Catalogue of the Severall Sects and Opinions in England and other Nations depicted on this Broadsheet of 1647 are the Anabaptists – shown third from the left on the bottom row – a non-conformist sect of religious separatists of which Mary's parents, Richard and Elizabeth Brookes, were adherents. *(British Museum)*

The Olde Ship Inn, High West Street, Dorchester
The oldest surviving pub in the town, built around 1600, the Old Ship, along with the Antelope Hotel, the Ship's great rival house, was doubtless one of the hostelries frequented by the teenage Mary while clandestinely indulging her young lover, of necessity avoiding those other establishments in the town owned by her parents.

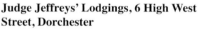

Judge Jeffreys' Lodgings, 6 High West Street, Dorchester

This Elizabethan styled house, now a restaurant, would have been one of the buildings familiar to Mary as she grew up, as would have been Jeffreys' past impact on the town, his name inextricably linked to one of the most notorious and controversial episodes in the history of Dorchester, known as the Bloody Assizes, over which he presided in the wake of the Monmouth Rebellion.

Antelope Walk, Dorchester

The entrance to Antelope Walk, now a popular cobbled shopping arcade, was once the frontage of the seventeenth century coaching inn. It was here that the Bloody Assizes were held in the Oak Room (now a tearoom) of the Antelope Hotel on the 5th September 1685. Judge Jeffreys is said to have had a secret tunnel connecting his lodgings in High West Street to the Oak Room, the passageway wide enough for three judges to walk side by side, allowing them safe passage after delivering an unpopular verdict. The recently publicised discovery of a tunnel beneath the shopping street in 2014 would seem to lend weight to the legend.

The English Dancing Master:

OR,

Plaine and easie Rules for the Dancing of Country Dances, with the Tune to each Dance.

LONDON,

Printed by *Thomas Harper*, and are to be sold by *John Playford*, at his Shop in the Inner Temple neere the Church doore. 1 6 5 1.

Title page of The Dancing Master (1st edition 1651)
As members of the aspiring commercial 'middle' class, Mary's parents were keen to add a polish to their daughter's social 'finish' by sending her for dancing lessons, then seen as one of the fashionable accomplishments of a refined young lady, and one of those social graces that was supposedly the mark of polite company, Accordingly, every fortnight, Mary attended a local dance school in Dorchester, presided over by a dancing master who would invariably have taught from a manual such as the one pictured above. However, after the classes were over, nights of frivolity and mirth ensued, marking the point at which Mary 'began to delight too much in the vanities of entertainment', yet her pleasure-seeking was later to extend beyond her after-hours dance class amusements.
(The Dancing Master, 1651-1728: An Illustrated Compendium by Robert M. Keller)

Fashion Plate - Costume à la Francaise
While there is no contemporary image of Mary in existence, in keeping with her widely denounced exuberance and love of frivolity, we can assume that she would have enjoyed the latest trends. This fashion plate from the 1690s shows a fashionable lady attired à la mode in the vogue of the late seventeenth century, which Mary would doubtless have striven to emulate in her own personal style of dress.

Hogarth's Marriage A-la-Mode: The Marriage Settlement

In order to curb their daughter's increasingly wayward inclinations, Mary's parents decided to 'dispose of her in Marriage as soon as possible', in the hopes that perhaps a husband would exercise more control over her than they had been able. However, as epitomised by Hogarth's satirical depiction, few arranged marriages were conducive to blissful connubiality, (note the two dogs, chained together in the bottom left corner, symbolising the binding woe of an unsuitable marriage) as was to be the case with the young man named Thomas Channing who began to pay court to the reluctant Miss Brookes, and to whom she was eventually coerced in matrimony. *(The National Gallery)*

Cruxton Manor

A family of noted local standing, the Channings, hailing from Maiden Newton, a parish eight miles north-west of Dorchester, actually came from the small hamlet of Cruxton, situated just south of the town, close to the River Frome. Richard Channing, Gentleman, was recorded as the owner of Higher 'Crookston' (an archaic spelling of Cruxton) in 1654, and the Channings

were known to have still been at the family property in 1743. At the age of 25, Thomas, having recently completed his apprenticeship, took over the grocer's shop which his father had established for his son to run in Dorchester. Now at a point in his life where he was expected to marry and settle down, Thomas' background, respectability and future prospects made him an ideal choice in the eyes of any would-be in-laws, never mind those who were looking to off-load an unruly, headstrong daughter. *(Image courtesy of the Maiden Newton Village Website www.maidennewton.info)*

Maiden Newton, Medieval Market Cross opposite The White Horse Inn

In Thomas Channing's day, Maiden Newton was a market town with a larger settlement, having had its own market and fair from the time of Henry III. In the image, the stub of the old Market Cross (dating to the fifteenth century) is still in its original position, opposite the *White Horse Inn* (now sadly demolished), one of the nine inns which Maiden Newton boasted up until the 1850s. The remains of the Medieval cross still endure however, though now removed from its original position in the middle of the road to the junction of Dorchester Road and Church Road, to prevent further damage by traffic after a vehicle crashed into it in the 1990s. *(Image courtesy of Dorset County Museum)*

The Town Pump Obelisk, head of South Street, Dorchester

While there is no exact record of the position of the Channing grocery shop in the town, in the Serious Admonitions to Youth we are told that en route to Mary's execution she was 'dragged' – that is taken in a cart – past her father's and her husband's houses; we know that the Brookes family home was located on the north side of High East Street, and according to *The Times* newspaper article penned by Thomas Hardy, Channing's Grocers apparently occupied the same street. In an area of competitive neighbouring retailers, it is reasonable to surmise that the premises would have been close to 'old' Dorchester's commercial centre, which occupied the area of South Street known as Cornhill, at its junction with High East Street, since medieval times the original site of Dorchester's market, with the site of the old market house, at the head of the street, now marked by a limestone obelisk erected in 1784 and formerly the site of the Town Pump.

Interior of a busy apothecary shop - Line engraving by Claude LeRoy (1712-1792)
Since Medieval times the increase in the establishment of apothecary shops in many towns and cities meant that any number of toxic substances were easily available for purchase. In evidence given at her trial, Mary was said to have purchased a farthing's worth of Mercury 'a piece about the bigness of a Walnut' from Mr Wolmington's Apothecary Shop in Dorchester.
(Image courtesy of Wellcome Library, London)

Druggist's jar for mercury pills, 1731-1770
While for centuries mercury was an essential component of many different medicines, such as diuretics, antibacterial agents, antiseptics, laxatives and widely used in the treatment of syphilis, the mercury-based remedies that the sick and ailing endured were hardly efficacious, as many patients died of mercury poisoning. The mercury pills that this jar once contained were in all likelihood made to a recipe developed by Augustin Belloste (1654-1730), which, though famous throughout Europe and in high demand as a

treatment for gout, kidney stones and bladder stones as well as for syphilis, nevertheless would have slowly poisoned those who unknowingly dosed themselves with the toxic medication.
(Wellcome Images)

Last Will & Testament of Thomas Channing

Mary supposedly administered the first of a possible three doses of mercury on Monday 16th April 1705: on Wednesday 18 April, with the increase of 'tormenting pains', Thomas Channing wrote his will, and may even have begun to suspect his wife, as tellingly he bequeathed his entire estate to his father, except for the 'one shilling' that he left to Mary 'having every good reason to give her no more.'
(Bristol Consistory Court Records ref B C/W/C Record 29, 1705)

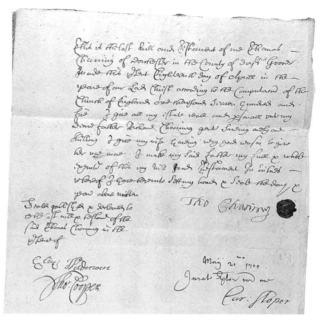

Thorncombe Wood, Puddletown Forest

This pocket of mixed ancient woodland and heath, itself part of the larger Puddletown Forest, is likely hiding place where Mary sought to conceal herself after her flight from Dorchester on the evening of Friday 20 April, the *Serious Admonitions to Youth* informing us that after Mary had left the safe house of a friend, she made for a parish about four miles from Dorchester and spent the best part of Saturday 'hiding in a neighbouring wood'. Her route would have traversed the dark heath on the western edge of the forest, Black Heath – Hardy's 'Egdon Heath' in *The Return of the Native*, with its stretch of old Roman Road which could be threatening to the lonely traveller, bolstered by tales of a phantom Roman centurion haunting the ancient route to Dorchester from Badbury Rings. *(Image courtesy of Chris Collins)*

Blue Plaque marking the site of Dorchester's first known gaol, at the junction of High Street East and Icen Way

Formerly known as 'Gaol Lane' this road led to Gallows Hill. Following her arrest on Sunday 21 April and return to Dorchester on the next day to face initial questioning and examination at a pre-trial hearing before Dorchester's Justices of the Peace, Mary was committed into custody, where she remained awaiting trial before the Summer Assizes which that year commenced in Dorchester on Thursday 26 July.

The Old Shire Hall, High West Street, Dorchester

The proceedings for the Assize courts in Dorchester were held at the Old Crown Court, located within the Old Shire Hall building. Howeve,r in Mary's day, cases would have been heard in the courtroom which stood previously on this site as the Grade I listed building we see in High West Street today (which incidentally is set to be transformed into a new historic justice-themed visitor attraction) was in fact built in 1796 during the reign of George III, the former Old Shire Hall having fallen into a shabby state of disrepair in 1769.

The Honourable Robert Price (1653-1733)

Mr Justice Price presided over Mary's trial held on Saturday 28 July 1705, the last day of the Dorchester Summer Assizes which had opened on the previous Thursday. An experienced jurist, Price's legal career began when he became attorney-general for South Wales in 1682, but he was a politician as well as a judge – serving as Member of Parliament for Weobley in Herefordshire, Price resigned the seat in favour of his elder son, Thomas, in 1702, upon being elevated to the bench as a Baron of the Exchequer by Queen Anne on her accession that year.

(National Library of Wales)

The Honourable ROBERT PRICE Esq.e one of the BARONS of his Majesties Court of EXCHEQUER 1711

Dorset Martyrs Memorial, created by Dame Elisabeth Frink

The execution site at Gallows Hill is today marked by the Dorset Martyrs Memorial. Created by Dame Elisabeth Frink and erected in 1986, the larger than life bronze statues of two martyrs facing a representation of Death commemorates the countless men and women – both Catholic and Protestant – who were executed on this spot for their adherence to their faith during the religious troubles of the sixteenth and seventeenth centuries.

Maumbury Rings, Dorchester
The site of Mary Channing's execution, the large circular earthwork, 85 metres in diameter, with a single bank and internal ditch and an entrance to the north east was a Neolithic henge, adapted by the Romans as an amphitheatre for the use of the citizens of Durnovaria – Roman Dorchester. The monument is now a public open space, and used for open-air concerts, festivals and re-enactments.

The execution of Anne Williams, from The Newgate Calendar

In a parallel to Mary Channing's fate, Anne Williams was the last woman to be burned at the stake in Gloucestershire; consigned to the flames on Friday, 13 April 1753, condemned for murdering her husband by poison. By the time Anne Williams was burnt at the stake, it had become common practice for the hangman to tie a rope around the prisoner's neck and strangle her, before the flames had reached high enough to burn her alive. The illustration of Anne's execution appearing in *The Newgate Calendar* would therefore suggest a certain amount of artistic licence, and adding to the shock value as it shows her fully conscious and praying, yet the mismanagement of many such executions did lead to instances of horrific live burnings, which was the fate that befell Mary Channing.

Catherine Hayes burnt for the murder of her husband.

Talois sculp.

Catherine Hayes being burnt for the murder of her husband

Another execution which was horribly botched, Catherine Hayes was all but burned to death after '...the executioner was foiled in an endeavour to strangle her by the burning of the rope'. Though sympathetic onlookers piled up the faggots around her, to hasten her end, the Newgate Calendar nevertheless reported that '...while she rent the air with her cries and lamentations ... she survived amidst the flames for a considerable time'. Catherine's suffering was brought to an end when she '... was finally killed by a piece of wood which was thrown at her head and dashed out her brains.'

St Mary's Church, Maiden Newton

The churchyard of St Mary's contains
the tombs (table style and other) of
well-known local people, like the
Channings, and included amongst
the many memorials in the church to
previous rectors and their families are
those to the Channings of Cruxton (in
the Jesus Chapel in the south transept
- right). Thomas Channing's body had
been laid to rest nearly a year prior
to his wife's execution – as soon as
the Coroner's inquest had been held,
following the autopsy carried out at
the behest of his father, after which
Thomas' remains were transferred
from Dorchester to Maiden Newton
for burial amongst his ancestors. It was
noted that the funeral procession on
24 April 1705 through the village to St
Mary's Church was accompanied by
sixty to eighty people on horseback,
Thomas and the Channing family
at large being so well respected in
the district. There would be no such
funeral rights or burial for Mary, who
'...in the sight of many thousands ...
was consumed to ashes.'

Thomas Hardy by Reginald Grenville Eves, 1923

The fate of Mary Channing was the inspiration for Hardy's ballad *The Mock Wife*, the renowned author and poet seemingly held by an enduring, and some would say grim fascination with Mary's story, recording some of the grislier details of his research about her execution in his Personal Notebooks. Hardy also harboured doubts over Mary's guilt, having '... examined more than once a report of her trial' he found 'no distinct evidence that the thoughtless, pleasure-loving creature committed the crime, while it contains much to suggest that she did not.' *(The National Gallery)*

Thomas Hardy statue, Dorchester

Occupying pride of place at the top of the High Street that the author knew so well, one of the most recognisable landmarks in Dorset's county town, a thoughtful looking bronze created by renowned sculptor Eric Henri Kennington, Hardy is depicted sitting on a tree stump with a book in his lap – it is said that the decision to sculpt Hardy seated was taken to compensate for the fact that he was known to be very short! Nevertheless, the statue is a testament to the impact that Hardy has had on the town, and the recognisable inspirations which he drew that were, and still are, instrumental in shaping the conceptions of Dorchester, and its inhabitants, to this day. The statue was unveiled on 2nd September 1931 by J.M. Barrie, the author of *Peter Pan* and a long-time close friend of Thomas Hardy.

Blue Plaque, Barclay's Bank, South Street, Dorchester

Many of the settings in Hardy's novels and poetry are inseparable from the places that inspired them, his work suffused with his native landscape of 'Wessex', his revival of the ancient Saxon name for the southwestern counties of England which Hardy described as 'a partly-real, partly dream-country'. Dorchester was the basis for the Casterbridge of his tales, the town itself figuring as prominently as the characters in his writing. An affirmation of which is the blue plaque affixed to the flint-faced building on South Street currently a Barclay's Bank, proudly proclaiming: 'This house is reputed to have been lived in by the Mayor of Casterbridge'. Mary Channing's execution is referenced by Hardy in *The Mayor of Casterbridge*.

Max Gate, outskirts of Dorchester

The austere but sophisticated Victorian town house, a short walk from the town centre of Dorchester, designed by Hardy, was his home from 1885 until his death in 1928. It was while Hardy was living at Max Gate, the house named after a nearby tollgate keeper called 'Mack', that *The Mock Wife* was written, some time between 25 January 1919, when he made a notebook entry on the subject, and July 1925 when Hardy sent the manuscript to his publisher, Macmillan. The poem was included in his 1925 collection entitled *Human Shows, Far Phantasies, Songs and Trifles*. As the title suggests, this was a somewhat miscellaneous set of poems, and the last to be published in Hardy's lifetime.

Love given over:

OR, A

SATYR

AGAINST THE

Pride, Luft, and Inconftancy, &c.

OF

WOMAN.

Amended by the AUTHOR.

LONDON,

Printed for R. *Bentley* and *J. Tonfon.*
1690.

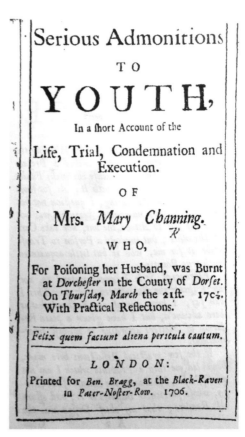

Serious Admonitions

TO

YOUTH,

In a fhort Account of the

Life, Trial, Condemnation and
Execution.

OF

Mrs. *Mary Channing.*

WHO,

For Poifoning her Husband, was Burnt
at *Dorchefter* in the County of *Dorfet.*
On *Thurfday,* March the 21ft. 17c¾.
With Practical Reflections.

Felix quem faciunt aliena pericula cautum.

LONDON:

Printed for *Ben. Bragg,* at the *Black-Raven*
in *Pater-Nofter-Row.* 1706.

Title page to Robert Gould's Love Given O'er: or the Satire on Woman, 1690

Gould was vitriolic in the misogynistic themes he pursued in his work, yet his misanthropic predilections were deeply entrenched in a society where the aberration of the murderess loomed large in the collective psyche. As such, Mary Channing, and others who were in 'defiance of wifely obedience' were perceived as posing a threat to masculine authority and patriarchal familial order that was the foundation upon which late seventeenth and early eighteenth century society was built, and the condemnation of female domestic homicide all the greater for that.

Title page to *Serious Admonitions to Youth* (abridged title)

The small fifty-two-page booklet, published in 1706 by Benjamin Bragg of the Black Raven in Paternoster Row, London, is made up of five letters, written at the publisher's request for an account of Mary Channing's background, crime and execution. Liberally interspersed with often lengthy pontifications concerning the 'hardening Nature of Sin' and the lessons to be learned from Mary's wicked life, although none of the letters in the published account are signed, it is clear from the details and information included that the writer was someone who was living in Dorchester at the time, and in view of the inclusion of his own (often lengthy) sermons, drawing on the spiritual aspect of these moralising missives, we can assume that the anonymous admonisher was a prominent clergyman in Dorchester.

Brookes Family graves, St Michael's churchyard, Stinsford

With regards to the vestiges of her familial ties, the graves of Mary's younger brother Thomas (above left) and his wife Martha and their son Edward (named on the same tombstone as his mother above right) can be found in the churchyard of St Michael's at Stinsford, a little less than two miles from Dorchester. While the details of monumental inscriptions in St Michael's graveyard show that Thomas died in 1749, in the 55th year of his age, the Stinsford Parish Registers however more accurately record his burial on May 15th 1748: born about 1693 he was therefore eight years or thereabouts Mary's junior. Thomas Brookes had settled in the hamlet of Bockhampton in the parish of Stinsford after his marriage to Martha (surname unknown) in about the year 1717 and taken up life as a yeoman farmer there. While only one of their sons is buried alongside them, the parish register shows that the couple had at least five children, all of whom were baptised into the Church of England at Stinsford, as was their Anabaptist father in his mid-twenties.

The grave marking the place of burial of Thomas Hardy's heart

It was at St Michael's that Thomas Hardy was also baptised, and while his ashes are interred in Poets' Corner in Westminster Abbey, his heart is buried in Stinsford churchyard, alongside the grave of his first wife Emma Lavinia Gifford who died in 1912, next to whom his second wife, Florence Dugdale Hardy is also interred; here too Hardy's parents were laid to rest. St Michael's is the 'Mellstock Church' so lovingly described in Under the Greenwood Tree.

the prosecution and defence witnesses testified, with the judge's seat on the other side of the room. While the similarities between Dorchester Crown Court and the Old Bailey are subject to supposition, before the introduction of gas lighting in the early nineteenth century, it is likely that similarly a mirrored reflector was placed above the bar, in order to reflect light from the windows onto the faces of the accused, thus allowing the court to examine their facial expressions and assess the validity of their testimony. In addition, there would be a sounding board placed over the dock in order to amplify their voices so that their testimony might be clearly heard. Seated at a table below the raised dais of the judge's bench were the clerks, lawyers and the writers who took the shorthand notes which formed the basis of the Proceedings, though in this respect it should be noted that a full transcription of Mary's trial has not survived. Though this is unfortunate, it comes as no real surprise; many assize court records prior to the nineteenth century have been lost. Also, while earlier records are less likely to have been kept than later ones, the clerks of assize sometimes destroying them when they ran out of space. It is further noted by the author of the *Serious Admonitions to Youth* that the testimonies put forth were 'The best that I could obtain', and when referring to the trial transcript, that 'an exact Account of which must not be expected, none having taken it complete'. Nevertheless the 'short Account of the Trial of Mary Channing, Widow, at the Assizes held at Dorchester, July the 26th, 27th, and 28th, 1705, before Judge Price' appearing in that publication is copious and thorough enough to give an insight into the legal proceedings and damning testimonies presented, in the face of which, though she put a spirited defence, Mary could not hope for acquittal.

It was little more than a 500 yard walk from the old Dorchester Gaol to the Crown Court. As Mary was escorted along High East Street, running into High West Street where the famous Corn Exchange clock now stands, with the early morning warmth of late July promising a sultry day, did she hold her head defiantly high, not turning to look at the faces of the onlookers, resisting a response to the taunts and jibes that must have been directed her way? Whether or not she dressed modestly for the occasion, her pregnancy may yet have been visible, adding to the tarnish with which her character had already been liberally applied. And all the principal players in her life and trial would already have taken up their places in courtroom – her parents and family and friends praying for a favourable outcome to the day as vehemently as the Channings wished to see her get her final comeuppance, with a guilty verdict handed down and the just punishment she so rightly deserved for the murder she was supposed to have committed.

The judicial process which Mary was about to face would be reliant on witness testimony, the most common source of evidence. After the clerk had read the charge, the prosecutor would present the case against Mary, followed by the witnesses who would testify under oath, after which Mary would be asked to state her case. Before 1898, defendants were not put on oath as this was thought to be a form of compulsion. Cross-examinations were conducted by the judge and defendant, or, if they were present, by the defence lawyer, though in Mary's case she had no such legal representation. Also it should be remembered that, prior to the early nineteenth century, there was no presumption of innocence, nor any right to remain silent. Defendants were expected to disprove the evidence presented against them and establish their own innocence, the assumption being that if a defendant was innocent, then they ought to be able to prove it...

Chapter 5

'The Trial held long...'

As the court assembled, everyone stood while they waited for Justice Price to take his seat on the bench. In his scarlet ermine lined robes and wearing a full-bottomed wig in the seventeenth century style, Price appeared as the 'face of justice', with the gilded royal coat of arms flashing its power from the wall behind him. While literacy levels were increasing amongst the population at large, the late seventeenth and early eighteenth centuries were still a visual culture. The importance of distinguishable symbolism was not lost on the judicial system, with the value of spectacle evoking awe from 'ordinary men', as asserted by Judge William Blackstone (1723-1780) in his Commentaries, 'the novelty and very parade' of a judge's appearance having 'no small influence on the multitude'.

Next, the jury were selected, whose names we do not know, but suffice to say it was ideally comprised of 'twelve good men and true' – there would be no female jurors until the Sex Disqualification (Removal) Act of 1919. The jury who would decide whether or not Mary was innocent or guilty would have been selected from the 'broad middling ranks' of society; drawn from the echelons of property holders, gentlemen, merchants, professionals, wealthier shopkeepers, tradesmen and artisans. It was also considered an advantage if jurors had prior knowledge of the background to a trial; any knowledge they had of the community (particularly of its more disreputable members) could come to bear when making decisions. However, in theory, they would have no prior connection with the case; possibly it was on these grounds that Mary challenged one of the jurors put forward. The matter of the jury selection settled, then, the indictment was read out, in English and, at Mary's request, repeated in Latin (proof of the level of her education) to which she pleaded 'not guilty'.

The council for the Queen were Sir John Darnell and Mr Serjeant Hooper, who in all probability was Nicholas Hooper of Caius College, Cambridge, who had been admitted to the inner temple in 1671, became a barrister 1678, then Sergeant at law in 1695; he opened the case for the prosecution. Mr Hooper confidently proceeded and:

'insisted on the Manner of her [Mary's] Life and Conversation, before, at, and after the Poisoning of her Husband, of which Fact he questioned not to prove her guilty by several Witnesses, nor did he doubt but the Jury would find her so.'

Though the scales of Justice were supposed to weigh blind and impartially, their balance could be off-set with the emphasis of conjectural evidence regarding a defendant's character, and thus would be no less effective in proving their guilt.

The first witness was called. This was Mr Francis Wadman, most probably the husband of Elizabeth Wadman who, along with one Thomas Cooper had witnessed the will that Thomas Channing had drawn up on his deathbed. After being sworn in, Wadman stated that on the Thursday and Friday before Thomas Channing was poisoned, a Mr Naile was at Mrs Channing's house and in her company; that they spent their time 'in eating, drinking and mirth'. That Mr Channing desired to 'lye' with him (Wadman) because Naile was to have his bed; but that Wadman refused, 'and showed his dislike at his kindness to Naile, whose company he thought would be prejudicial to him'. But that the same evening Mr Channing did come into his chamber after he was in bed 'and brought a pillow with him to lye with his apprentice; but that he hindered him from it and admitted him into his own bed'. As Wadman continued with his testimony, he stated that Mrs Channing, her husband, Naile and himself went on a trip to Burton where they 'ate, drank, and were merry'. From there, the party moved on to Charminster, just a mile and a half outside of Dorchester, 'where they did the like'. Returning to Wadman's testimony, he further related that, as obviously they were so close to home, Mrs Channing entreated Naile 'to return and lye at her house', as he had done two nights before, and that Mr Channing encouraged the same, and return they all did.

It was Mr Naile himself who was sworn in as the next witness and he confirmed that in the Easter week lately gone, he had gone to Dorchester to see Mr Channing, his old school fellow, and that he had been made welcome in the Channing house by Thomas and Mary likewise, 'who desired him to lodge there' and that he accepted her kindness. Confirming the facts as Wadman had presented them, namely the jaunts to Burton and Charminster, on being asked 'if he lay by himself' Naile said that he did, 'but that Mrs Channing came into his chamber in the morning, and made a noise, by pulling out her drawers, with which he awoke, and, seeing her there, asked her what she had got'. Mary replied 'a bottle of that which is good' and brought it to the bedside where they both drank. This she did every morning during his stay, but being pressed to tell if there was any greater familiarity between them, Naile unwillingly said that 'he did kiss her as she sat on the bed'. At this point, Justice Price advised Mary that she might interrogate the witness herself, and after directing several questions to Naile, she began to give her own account of their conversation, however on being directed by Price that this discourse was unnecessary as 'that evidence having done her no harm, as to the poisoning of her husband' Mary desisted with her cross-examination.

The next witness called was Mary's young lover, though frustratingly in the available account he is not named. Possibly the father of the child that Mary was carrying, he stated that *after* her marriage to Thomas Channing he was with Mary at an ale-house in the town and that she there offered him the gift of a watch, but that he had refused it. Being asked by the counsel 'if he did not [l]atter accept of it, how long he kept it, and what watch it was, if Gold, or Silver?' he admitted that latterly he did accept the said gift, 'but knew not what metal it was, nor how long he kept it'. Price again advised Mary that she might interject here, and she told the court that she had given the witness a gold watch, but had done so 'jestingly', not expecting him to keep it, also that while she had been on remand in prison she had 'sent for it, and had it restored again.'

Thinking that the testimony of the first two witnesses was sufficient to give the court an account of her life, just before the fact, the Counsel now moved 'to prove her guilty of the poisoning'.

Amy Clavel was now called to the stand; she was the shop assistant who had served Mary on the day she had purchased the poison from Mr Wolmington's apothecary shop. Her sworn testimony ran that on 16 April last, the prisoner at the bar came into her master's shop at about four o'clock in the afternoon and had asked for some 'ratsbane'. Clavel related how she had told Mary that there was none in stock, but that there was some mercury if she would prefer to purchase that instead, though she was unable to find this in the absence of her master. She told the court that she, the prisoner, found it (the mercury) herself 'and took a piece about the bigness of a walnut' for which she paid a farthing. Clavel went on to say that when she had questioned her customer as to what she had wanted the mercury for, Mary had replied ' to draw a picture of a man', whereupon she put it in her bosom and left the shop. Though this last alleged statement of Mary's seem strange on the face of it, mercury indeed had many uses. As well as a poison used in pest control – and obviously in murder! – amongst other uses, mercury was employed in silversmithing, the basis for Mary's brother's failed defence mentioned earlier, but in the seventeenth century and indeed right up to the modern day, it was also used extensively by artists in making the red pigment vermilion, achieved by mixing and heating one part mercury with one part white sulphur. Painters at this time were used to making their own pigments, so would have purchased mercury for such a purpose, therefore Mary's response was simply a plausible excuse for wanting to purchase the substance i.e. to paint a picture of a man.

The next witness called had been a customer in Mr Wolmington's apothecary shop on the day that Mary had made her purchase. Mr Henry Meggs was clearly the subject of a high-spirited jest on Mary's part, because he said that Mrs Channing had asked him 'if he would be her taster? And offered him the mercury, which she had in her hand; which he took and was about to taste' until the shop assistant hurriedly intervened and told him that if he did it would poison him. Understandably, Mr Meggs was not amused as he remonstrated, 'What, would you give me poison? I had rather you would give me a drachm of innocence'; a drachm was a unit of weight formerly used by apothecaries, equivalent to 60 grains or one eighth of an ounce. Mr Meggs concluded his testimony by saying that he left, presumably in high dudgeon, while Mary was still in the shop.

Mr Meggs' account was confirmed by Robert Martin, described as 'a lad' who had also been in the apothecary shop at the same time, and who next took the stand. He said that the shop assistant intimated to Mary that she would prefer for her customer to remain in the shop until her master, Mr Wolmington, returned – perhaps she was concerned about selling the poison to Mary in the absence of her employer – but that in the witness's hearing, Mary had refused to wait as she wanted the mercury presently 'to paint something which would otherwise be spoiled'. This statement was rather telling, as, while arsenic was certainly a component of paints at this time, Mary had originally gone shopping for 'ratsbane', inferring a need for a pesticide, rather than the purchase of something for artistic purposes. As Mary proceeded to serve herself, searching the shop's stock for what she required, on finding a box she suspected contained white lead, (confusingly the white crystalline solid form of mercuric chloride resembles that of white lead) the assistant managed to convince her to the contrary by showing her the box that actually contained white lead; satisfied, Mary took the mercury from the first box instead. Robert Martin had some further, some would say damning, testimony to add to his account, however, concerning Mary's younger brother who was apparently standing in the shop doorway at the time. Though we know Mary had at least six brothers, in all probability the boy in the doorway of the apothecary shop was Thomas Brookes – the burial records of the Stinsford Parish Registers confirm that Thomas died in 1749 in the 55th year of his age, therefore born about 1693 he was eight years or thereabouts Mary's junior. When young Thomas asked his sister: 'Our Mall, ['Mall' is an old fashioned diminutive of 'Mary'] what are you going to do; will you put poison in the sugar? If you do some person or other will poison themselves with it,' according to Robert Martin, Mary's sharp and testy remonstration was, 'Kiss my arse, you young rogue; if you don't hold your tongue I will knock you down.' She then left the shop and went home.

As matters stood, in the face of such testimonies, the prospect of Mary's acquittal was looking shaky and the testimony of the next witness only added fuel to the fire.

Elizabeth Cosins was the Channing's maid, and a particularly useful witness for the prosecution as she was well placed to observe the internal domestic goings on of the Channing household. Elizabeth stated that on 17 April, in the morning, Mary Channing, her then mistress, was busy preparing breakfast for her husband. After boiling some milk with rice, Mary 'came to her in the shop and bid her call her master out of the cellar' which she did accordingly. That Thomas Channing went into the kitchen as bidden and a little later Elizabeth followed him. Overhearing her master say that his milk was 'gristy' and that he could not eat it, Elizabeth said that her mistress had persuaded him to try again. However on his refusal Mary took the dish from him saying 'this is gristy indeed' and threw it into the House of Office. That Mary then washed the dish and took her husband some more, and upon her asking him how he liked it he replied 'very well' but that he could not eat much. Elizabeth then recounted how after about half an hour had passed Thomas Channing began to vomit and was 'very sick'. She further related the instance of the dog licking up the vomit, and 'being taken in a vomiting likewise'.

It would seem apparent from the cases of other condemned poisoners that animals either accidentally ingesting or being deliberately fed supposedly poisonous substances was commonly held as a reliable indicator of foul play, still employed well over a century after Mary Channing was found guilty. In the case of the serial poisoner, Mary Bateman, infamously known as 'The Yorkshire Witch' who was hanged before an estimated crowd of twenty thousand people from York's New Drop gallows in 1809, at her trial, evidence based on such methodology was presented by the surgeon attending on her last victim, Rebecca Perigo. Incidentally, Bateman was tried and convicted on a single count of murder, but we can say with a measure of certainty that she killed at least three others, and in all probability was responsible for many more deaths that escaped detection. An artful fraudster and confidence trickster she had managed to evade prosecution for more than two decades by the time of her eventual arrest. The surgeon involved in the Bateman case, a Mr Chorley, conducted a number of tests which were taken as proof that poison had been ingested, the poison supplied by Bateman supposedly having been incorporated by the victim herself into puddings consumed over the course of a week. Mary Bateman was something of a canny operator; in contriving the long distance poisoning of her victims, she supplied the necessary substances under the guise of benign powders, either medicinal in nature or intended to assist in the removal of a curse, or 'evil wish', and those making use of her services, and paying a high price into the bargain, effectively dosed themselves, willingly so, in the misplaced belief that all their problems would soon be solved. The lives of an entire family, who like the Perigos had similarly sought Mary Bateman's assistance, were only spared after the fortuitous and timely appearance of an article detailing her arrest appeared in a regional newspaper. With regards to Chorley's tests for the presence of poison, he firstly suggested that some of the flour used by the victim in the preparation of the last pudding be made up into a paste and fed to a chicken to see what harm might befell the bird. Whether or not the flour used was untainted, or the test subject had a lucky escape, the chicken suffered no ill effects from the experiment. However, a cat which had been experimentally fed some of the last cooked pudding (by Rebecca Perigo's suspicious neighbours) had died immediately; though surprisingly Mr Chorley's suspicions were clearly not aroused at that time, he taking no further steps to arrange for an autopsy on Rebecca Perigo's body. Chorley did however later perform an autopsy on the body of a dog which had died as a result of being fed pills and a solution made from some honey that Rebecca had also been directed to take by Bateman – ironically if she were to feel unwell. This time Chorley found the presence of poison in the animal's stomach, a conclusion invariably reached when any darkening or discolouration was found to be present.

As a further demonstration of the continued reliance of this evidential indicator, another Yorkshire housewife and convicted poisoner, Ursula Lofthouse, was hanged alongside two other convicted murderers in York on 6 April 1835, she having poisoned her husband with two pennyworth of arsenic purchased from her local apothecary. Though it was initially assumed that her husband had contracted cholera, the presumption of poisoning was soon reinforced by the swift demise of four chickens after the birds had pecked at some of Robert Lofthouse's vomit, evidence of arsenic being later found in the craw of each. Likewise, the rumours which had begun to spread about the Edinburgh poisoner, William Bennison who murdered his wife in 1850, were initially aroused after the death of two of his neighbour's dogs, which had eaten cooked potatoes put out by Bennison on the night of his wife's death.

Though the credence placed on such circumstantial evidence might point to some dubious verdicts being reached, in the face of the relative infancy of the field of forensic toxicology, it would have been easy to sway a jury, and though the methods used were rudimentary and unsophisticated, such evidence presented during a poisoning trial in the early 1700s would have nevertheless have proved damning.

Further testimonies with regard to the subsequent ill effects Thomas Channing suffered after eating his breakfast (and the suspicion of poisoning) were presented. Bernard Hamlin swore that he saw Mr Channing eating the milk and that he had heard Thomas complain that his breakfast tasted 'gristy' and 'the rest that the maid [Elizabeth Cosins] had sworn'. Hamlin added that he saw Mrs Channing wash the dish at the cock, presumably at the public 'cock' or water pump; it is very unlikely that the Channings would have had a cistern fed supply laid on as privately piped water was uncommon and usually only available to the larger, more affluent households at this time. And tellingly, this was probably one of those jobs that ordinarily Mary would have felt beneath her and would normally have been delegated to their servant. Hamlin was also amongst those who saw Thomas Channing vomit; he had 'asked him if he was well before he ate the milk, and he told him he was.'

At this point, the first witness was again recalled – Francis Wadman who had earlier testified as a member of the party who had travelled with the Channings and Mr Naile on their junket to Burton and Charminster. It was Wadman, who on seeing 'the vomit lye on the ground' immediately suspected 'Mr C to be poisoned, and sent for a doctor, and told him the like, who gave him medicine accordingly.'

Yet more damaging evidence was to issue forth from the witness stand. Mr Wolmington, the proprietor of the apothecary shop, stated that in a private conversation between himself and Mary, he had 'told the prisoner at the bar that he thought her guilty of poisoning her husband and that if she would confess it to him he would serve her as far as possible'. According to Wolmington, Mary had fallen on her knees and entreated him 'for Christ

Jesus sake to not say anything of it'. Here Mary was again allowed to interject, claiming 'that she never said these words, nor did she kneel down at all,
but only stooped to tie up a shoe', yet it is clear from the account of the trial
that this assertion, along with her many other 'excuses' were taken by the
court to have no validity. If she was not already damned in the eyes of the
jurors, the medical evidence in the case was yet to be presented.

In his testimony, the doctor who was called by Francis Wadman to attend
on Thomas Channing declared that on being sent for, he gave Mr Channing
oil and water to cleanse his stomach of the poisonous matter 'which had
some good effect and he appeared something better'. He continued that he
visited him frequently but after Wednesday – the following day after Thomas
had eaten some of his 'gristy' breakfast' – that his patient grew worse and,
finding the poison had 'seized his lungs', he advised Thomas' friends that
the prognosis was hopeless and that he would inevitably die. On the Sunday,
his patient's pulse was quite gone and about nine o'clock Thomas Channing
died with a 'hisking cough like a rotten sheep'. On Monday the doctor
'caused the body to be opened' at the insistence of Richard Channing who
had pressed for an autopsy to be carried out on his son. After performing
this, he found 'the bottom of his stomach, lungs and part of his liver black
and several spots in his guts which he believed to be the effects of poison'.

As mentioned earlier, reliance on such rudimentary toxicological
evidence was all that was available at the time. It would be forty-seven
years before a court accepted the first early forensic tests of Dr Anthony
Addington, presented in the case of Mary Blandy as evidence in a trial
of murder by poisoning, in 1752. In this instance, the poison employed
by Mary Blandy to kill her father was arsenic, and while Addington was
not a chemist but the Blandy family physician, his conclusions were based
on observational analysis and physical tests – for instance, when he put
a sample of the powder given to Mary's father into cold water, part of it
remained on the water's surface while most of it stayed on the bottom
undissolved – the same results apparent when a known sample of arsenic
was similarly tested. Additionally, when Addington tossed the powder onto
a red-hot piece of iron, it did not burn, but sublimated, in other words,
transformed directly from a solid to the gaseous state, rising up in gar-
lic-smelling white clouds – just as arsenic did. Addington argued that these
results were conclusive and proved that the powder employed was in fact
arsenic. Though these forensic tests were in no way definitive, nor specific
to arsenic alone, the jury were nevertheless convinced and, agreeing with
Addington's findings, Mary Blandy was sentenced to death and hanged on

6 April 1752 in the castle yard at Oxford, though as a footnote to her case, incredibly she was seemingly more concerned with the preservation of her modesty than with her impending execution, her last request that, for the sake of decency, she should not be hoisted too high, lest the young men in the crowd look up her skirts!

Returning to the sultry atmosphere of Dorchester's Crown Court, as the trial 'held long', Mary, who was at this point 'quite spent' was granted the request for some refreshment, a glass of water, or small beer. After she had taken a drink, the *Serious Admonitions to Youth* states that many more witnesses were called, some 'to confirm several particulars of what these had deposed; some to give an account of Mr Channing's illness; others to prove her [Mary's] flight', yet there was one witness whose sworn testimony was in support of Mary. While the identity of this witness is not known, other than that she was female, she nevertheless testified that 'the prisoner told her Mr Channing had poisoned himself by handling some poison in his own shop, before any persons suspected him to be poisoned' – crucial testimony indeed from a defence point of view. Though the outcome in mercury toxicity depends on the form of the mercury compound and the severity of exposure, fatality is usually the result of severe exposure to mercuric salt. Mild exposure to inorganic (elemental mercuric salt) resulting from skin absorption through limited handling *can* result in a complete recovery. However, as this was a circumstance of which the jury would of course have been entirely ignorant at the time, this testimony could therefore have carried heavily in Mary's favour. As to the truth of the matter, whether or not this witness was faithfully reiterating an actual conversation, the fact remained that this evidence was based on an assertion of the accused and therefore carried little weight. Though Thomas Channing's symptoms would seem to indicate an acute case of mercury poisoning, this did not automatically make Mary culpable, other than in biased public opinion and, as Judge Price would have been careful to point out later in his summing up, the jury would need to be confident beyond doubt that the administration of the poison that had supposedly caused the death of Thomas Channing was with the knowledge and contrivance of Mary, and that it had been done in the expectation of causing his death.

Though she had no recourse to Counsel of her own, Mary very capably conducted her own defence. Asking 'many proper questions' of the witnesses, and herself 'answering several things they said' she called as a principal witness for herself one John Whiten. Again, as with the conversational evidence presented by the unidentified witness above,

Whiten's testimony was crucial in supporting Mary's not guilty plea, particularly with regard to the procurement of the poison supposedly employed to kill her husband. Whiten swore that:

> 'on the 16th April last he came to Dorchester and about four in the afternoon went to Mrs Channing's shop, bought of her one pound of sugar, half a pound of raisins, and asked for some Ratsbane; but she having none, fetcht [sic] him some mercury from the next shop, for which he gave her a penny.'

It would not have been unusual at this time to go into a grocery shop and ask for rat poison as this would have been carried in addition to the full range of other household comestibles stocked. The stumbling point came however when Mary's witness was questioned as to the quantity of mercury obtained, Whiten replying 'about the bigness of his finger', this statement supported by Whiten's daughter who had accompanied her father and swore almost the same as his testimony.

The testimony of Whiten and his daughter certainly supported Mary's having valid pretext for the purchase of the poison, other than that of the intent to murder Thomas Channing, and was certainly her best hope of acquittal, taken in conjunction with Thomas Channing supposedly having been responsible for his own demise by handling poison himself in his own shop. But it fell short of the measure, literally. Mr Justice Price instructed Mary to take note that her witnesses were mistaken about the quantity, the prior evidence given against her affirming that the poison obtained was as 'big as a walnut', while the evidence supporting her claim stated 'no bigger than the top of a finger'. Though she must have been tired at this point, after hours of concentrating on every detail of the evidence presented against her, questioning and counter questioning, Mary still had her wits about her, and put forward to his Lordship that there were indeed 'nuts of several sizes, and that the bigness of the nut was not at all described by the evidence; and so the quantities of her evidence, and that of the Queen [the prosecution] might be the same.' However, even if Mary's principal witness had been more exact in the quantity of poison he described, Thomas Channing's father was poised and 'had persons enough in court to invalidate their testimony, by giving such an account of them as their past actions deserved' – at this time, there were no rules governing how evidence was obtained. Not surprisingly, the consensus was that the weight of evidence presented by the prosecution in this case was irrefutable.

Nevertheless, Mary continued undaunted, calling many other witnesses, 'and made such an extraordinary defence for herself that the Judge declared he thought himself not capable of making a better [one]'. In variance to the prevalent contemporary chauvinistic attitude to female criminality, Justice Price's admiration counted for much, and indeed was in itself impartial and not grudgingly bestowed. In a moralising climate where it was held that while women were 'naturally much more amiable, tender and compassionate than the other sex, [they] become, when they pervert the dictates of nature, more remorseless and cruel, and can conceive and execute the most diabolical of crimes', this supposition summed up the feeling of the age and Mary's presumed guilt was bolstered by this universal view. While murder was representative of the ultimate crime, a murder committed by a woman was regarded as wholly more shocking. A situation in which a woman was exposed as a murderer violated the expectations of femininity and turned the world upside down. And there is a sense that the law was harsher upon a female killer than a male, she having outraged the societal norm. Yet while women were regarded as the inferior sex, legally passing all they owned, along with their autonomy, to their husbands with their wedding vows, in a court of law, however, women who stood accused like Mary were nevertheless tried as individuals.

Though Mary had amply demonstrated her grasp of the proceedings, as exemplified by the praise given her by Justice Price, if she had had the benefit of an able counsel, the outcome may yet have been very different. After denying the murder charge on Mary's behalf, cross-examining the witnesses, capitalising on the testimony of John Whiten and his daughter, as well as the assertion that Thomas Channing had accidentally poisoned himself, he may well have challenged the evidence given by the likes of Bernard Hamlin; for example, if he was present in the grocery shop at the time, did he have a clear view of the kitchen? And with regard to the ample testimonies concerning Mary's purchasing poison, he would have pointed out that this alone was not proof of the intent to use it in a malign way. Nevertheless, they may have been hard put to persuade the jury of their client's innocence. The fact remained that in the face of the medical evidence presented, and, though mostly circumstantial, the remainder of the detrimental testimonies, there would have been a slim chance of an acquittal for Mary, whose character was already shadowed by an irretrievable eclipse of the worst kind.

Mr Justice Price, in his summing up of the case, would have reminded the jury that to bring in a guilty verdict they had to satisfy themselves on three points – that Thomas Channing had died from poisoning, that the poison had been administered with the knowledge and contrivance of Mary and that it had been done in the expectation of causing Thomas Channing's death. Yet after only half an hour spent in deliberation, the jury returned and brought in a verdict of guilty. The prisoner was removed from the dock.

After a brief adjournment, in the evening sentence was passed upon Mary. Accordingly, Judge Price placed the black cloth sentencing cap over his powdered wig and proceeded to pass sentence of death; yet Mary had one last card to play. When the Clerk of the Arraigns asked 'Mary Channing, what have you to say, why immediate execution should not be awarded against you?' Mary revealed what may have already been common knowledge; she 'pleaded her belly' – in other words, she announced to the court that she was pregnant.

Chapter 6

The Most Earnest Plea...

U nder English common law, 'pleading the belly' permitted women in the later stages of pregnancy to be reprieved of their death sentences until after the delivery of the child. The plea did not constitute a defence and could only be made after a guilty verdict had been passed. Verification of the claimant's condition was determined by what was termed as a 'jury of matrons', customarily drawn from the women observing the proceedings in the courtroom. If found to be 'quick with child' (that is, the movements of the foetus could be detected), a reprieve would be granted until after the birth, after which the sentence of death was reinstated. No pregnant woman was executed, as in doing so the life of the innocent party would be killed along with the guilty mother.

Obviously, this was a popular ploy to delay execution and many capitally convicted women between the ages of twelve and fifty therefore claimed to be with child: during the first quarter of the eighteenth century; at the Old Bailey alone, thirty-eight per cent of the women sentenced to death during that period entered such a plea – on one occasion, four women found guilty in a single trial all claimed they were pregnant.

Based on the tentative date of conception calculated in Chapter 3, working backwards from the birthdate of Mary's son on 19 December 1705, at the time of her trial Mary would have been somewhere around four months into her pregnancy, though of course, for the reasons conjectured in the same earlier chapter, Mary's pregnancy may have been further along. Naturally 'pleading the belly' was a judicial reprieve that was open to abuse. In Daniel Defoe's novel *Moll Flanders*, written in 1721, one character successfully pleads her belly despite being 'no more with child than the judge that tried [her]'. In such cases, even if the condemned mother's condition was visibly apparent, of course appearances could be contrived. Various strategies would be employed to hoodwink the court – the simplest, as described by 'Captain' Alexander Smith in his *General and True History of the Lives and Actions of the Most Famous Highwaymen* (1714) was 'cramming a Pillow in her Petticoat to make her look big', though there was also 'the old stratagem of drinking new Ale very plentifully, to make her swell'. However, while

these ploys might have deceived the judge and (all male) jury, nevertheless any woman who had contrived a sham pregnancy would have to face
a 'jury of matrons'. Defined as a 'prudent and virtuous, motherly woman,
also one of the grave women that have the over-sight of children in an
Hospital' twelve such women would have been empanelled to confirm the
pregnancy, though needless to say this was just another aspect of the judicial
system open to abuse. The practice of selecting a jury of matrons from the
courtroom observers opened up the opportunity for planting sympathetic
accomplices in the public gallery, assuring a favourable outcome, causing
one eighteenth century commentator to complain that female felons would
have 'Matrons of [their] own Profession ready at hand, who, right or wrong,
bring their wicked Companions quick with Child to the great Impediment
of Justice'. Invariably, however, on the occasions when such a plea was made,
this would cause a ripple of consternation throughout the women present in
the court. The prospect of their being selected to perform the examination
was understandably a discomforting one and in anticipation of their reaction
and a hasty exodus, it was not unknown for a judge to order the bailiffs to
lock the courtroom doors, in case the jury of empanelled matrons tried to
escape their duty; in many instances the selection must have been coercive
as such examinations were decidedly distasteful affairs.

In Mary's case, to verify her plea, Judge Price would have ordered the
sheriff to empanel the necessary jury of matrons, sworn in and charged
to inquire 'whether the prisoner was quick with child?' Though ideally
the matrons selected would exhibit the prudence and virtues previously
described, frequently the wives of court personnel and of course those often
reluctant female spectators watching the trial were co-opted. Several tests
were employed, though their reliability was debatable: feeling the prisoner's
belly and squeezing the breast for any sign of lactation were often as unde-
pendable as the presumed expertise of the 'matrons' selected to conduct
them. In the case of Mary's plea, after being escorted to a closed room, as for
the sake of common decency the matrons conducted their intimate examination in private, it was pronounced that Mary's claim was indeed founded.

While of course such examinations could not have detected the condition
of those who had only recently conceived, in theory, the very early stages
of pregnancy, prior to the foetus 'quickening', did not qualify for a stay of
execution anyway. Quickening was the crucial factor; as a rule women did
not consider themselves to be truly pregnant until the foetus 'quickened',
or reached the point at which the mother could feel the first movements of
the child she was carrying. This was because most people believed that the

foetus did not receive a soul until the time when it could be felt to move and without a soul, the foetus was not deemed a real 'person' or even considered to be 'alive'. This interpretation of *ensoulment* – the belief in the moment at which a human being gains a soul – occurring at a particular stage in an unborn child's development, did not change until the nineteenth century, when Pope Pius IX decided that souls entered the embryo at conception. And one such unfortunate case which occurred prior to this change of attitude in dogma was that of Christian Murphy, executed on 18 March 1789 at Newgate for counterfeiting silver coins. Like Mary Channing, Christian had 'pleaded her belly' after sentence of death had been passed on her and though her claim was verified, the matrons who examined her concluding that '... it was their opinion that she was with child, and has been so a short time...' nevertheless as she was '... not quick with child...' her execution went ahead accordingly. Pertinent to Mary's notable fate as the last woman burned at the stake in Dorset, Christian Murphy was incidentally the last woman in England to be burned at the stake. Nevertheless, in some instances late applications were considered, as was the case with Sophia Pringle in 1787. Convicted after a sensational trial for forging power of attorney, she claimed that she was pregnant just two days before she was due to be hanged and was brought back to court to make her plea. However, when she was found to be 'not quick with child' her execution went ahead before huge crowds, who witnessed her acute distress, fainting and raving, forcing her to be seated in a chair on the scaffold. Another late application, and one that was considered particularly unfortunate, was that of Elizabeth Hughes, convicted of horse-theft, a capital offence, at the Oxford Assizes of 1726; she miscarried just after the jury found her guilty, and : '...thereby lost the benefit of pleading her belly'.

As for Mary Channing, after the verification of her pregnancy, she was subsequently remanded back to prison, to await the birth of her child. Though she had gained a few extra months of life, after the delivery she would automatically be executed on the next 'hanging day'. As any accused person would, Mary must have clung to the hope of acquittal to the very end of the trial; the death sentence must have fallen on her as a heavy blow. The gravity of her situation now hitting home, Mary's 'first thoughts of death appeared dreadful to nature, and shocked her whole frame of her mind'. Yet, taking solace from the postponement of her execution, she soon composed herself, and her hopes were further raised by the possibility of obtaining a pardon. Some fortunate women awarded a reprieve on pleading their belly would sometimes later have their sentences commuted to imprisonment.

Though transportation was an option at this time, it was not easily arranged, The Transportation Act legitimising transportation as a direct sentence not introduced until 1717; and some fortunate women would even be subsequently granted a pardon and they after all regained their liberty.

On the Friday following her conviction, Mary's mother came to visit her in gaol, to let her daughter know that the family were doing everything in their power to obtain a pardon for her. During the reign of Queen Anne, judges themselves could not commute or pardon convicted prisoners; their power limited them only to reprieves, or temporary relief, while the monarch decided their fate. The power of pardon was a royal prerogative of mercy available to monarchs of the United Kingdom, though pardoning also served to satisfy the proletariat's expectations of justice, regardless of the letter of the law. The Bloody Code, the name given by historians to the English legal system from the late seventeenth century to the early nineteenth century, is known as such because of the huge numbers of crimes for which the death penalty could be imposed. Based heavily on its provisions for capital punishment, in 1688, the death penalty was the standard punishment for about fifty crimes, yet while the laws of the time allowed for punishment by death, the number of executions did not equal the number of indictments. For instance, only ten percent of those indicted in London in the period 1700–1750 were actually hanged. Instead of carrying out the death penalty consistently for every crime that allowed for it, the prerogative of English kings and queens to grant pardons was a means of keeping potential criminals in a state of uncertainty, with the principle aim being social control, though this selectively merciful approach also served to soften the strict emphasis on cruelty which the Bloody Code widely engendered – after all, had the indiscriminate use of the death penalty for the full range of crimes listed ever been adhered to, this would have made for a judicial system which advocated the death of more criminals than those who fell victim to purely homicidal criminals themselves.

Accordingly, at the end of each assize circuit, judges would submit a 'circuit pardon' or 'circuit letter', which was a list of those prisoners whom the judge felt to be worthy of a pardon. These letters would be sent to the Chancery, which usually approved the judge's recommendations – but of course, whether or not Judge Price had indeed complied such a list and included the names of any of those whose case he had heard at the Dorchester assize, Mary's name did not appear. So she had to rely upon her Brookes relations to shift for her. With regard to successfully obtaining a pardon, the status and respectability of the condemned were of paramount importance. If the prisoner could not rely upon his or her own status, then he or she could turn to a respected community member and beg for a supporting testimonial. Needless to say, Mary's tarnished reputation presented a definite obstacle, yet her elder brother waited upon the judge presiding at Wells, the last venue on the Western circuit for the summer assizes, and presented him with a petition signed by several upstanding Gentlemen of the County. Richard Channing had been equal in his energies, however, and to insure against the possibility of the guilty verdict being overturned in the eventuality that his daughter-in-law was granted a pardon, he took it upon himself to present his own petition 'for a fair representation of the case to the Queen', incredibly signed by some of those same Gentlemen who had affixed their seal in support of Mary's pardon. But as Richard Channing had additionally secured 'a great number of other Gentlemen' as signatories, the efforts of Mary's brother came to nothing. Yet the Brookes family still tried. In desperation, Mary's mother had addressed an honourable lady on her daughter's account, but was told that the case was 'too black for her to appear in, with any honour or honesty'. When a pardon was obtained, the members of the elite who assisted the prisoner in getting off enhanced their own reputation and status, but in cases such as Mary's, where no such social cachet was attached, the appeal was limited. For her father's part, in attempting to secure a pardon for his daughter, Richard Brookes used his utmost endeavours, travelling to London to present a petition for pardon to the Queen, but this was all to 'little purpose'.

While strident efforts were being made by Mary's family and friends to preserve her body, equally industrious endeavours were being made on the part of Mr Hutchins, Dorchester gaol's Ordinary (that is clergyman), with regards to Mary's spiritual redemption, as he was resolved on the salvation of Mary's soul. The Reverend Richard Hutchins was rector of All Saints parish church in Dorchester between 1693 and 1734. As Dorchester gaol fell within this parish, he also acted as the prison chaplain, and it was Hutchins' duty to provide spiritual guidance to those of his flock who were incarcerated, with a pressing responsibility to those prisoners who were condemned to death. Hutchins 'spared no pains in admonitions, exhortations or other means' to bring Mary 'to a true sense of her condition, and an un-resigned repentance'. It would have been his paramount concern to see that Mary came to terms with her immoral conduct and her guilt, her confession being essential in preparing for her salvation. Yet the role of the Ordinary in obtaining a confession as a way of underlining and legitimising the Court's decision was also fundamentally important from the judicial point of view; in seeking positive statements of guilt to a particular crime, this justified the death sentence and those criminals accepting the judgment of the jury, coming to terms with their guilt and confessing their crimes also conformed to the omnipresent moral overtones of the times Confession was indispensable proof of the sincerity of one's repentance, forming part of the rigorous self-examination which was the necessary precondition of spiritual re-acceptance, for the criminal who died without acknowledging his crime was damned. Yet in some instances, pride and human nature being what it is, an element of self-aggrandisement was at play, Ordinaries garnering admiration for their diligence and efforts in confronting the most hardened of criminals, attending on the condemned in spite of the endemic typhus outbreaks all too common in eighteenth century prisons, and prone to exaggerate the bad behaviour of malefactors to emphasise the marked improvement brought about under their care.

Hutchins got Mary various books to read that he felt appropriate to her situation, and while he earnestly recommended 'serious reading', though Mary outwardly complied and read several of the books, exasperatingly to Hutchins, to some of the texts she paid no more concern than she would have 'a play or a ballad'. The Reverend also encouraged her to come to chapel and although Mary confessed to other sins, she maintained throughout her innocence of the crime for which she was convicted – perhaps under the misguided belief, instilled in her by others, that if her confession was not forthcoming then the sentence of death would not be carried out. This misleading presumption was grounded upon a supposed reprieve granted some sixty years earlier to a person found guilty of the same crime yet 'against whom the evidence were not very clear' they thus had escaped the flames – and presumably why there is no record of their execution. Frustratingly, there is no record either of the woman apparently burnt at the stake mentioned in John Hutchins' *The History and Antiquities of the County of Dorset* – the author, who incidentally was the son of the Reverend Richard Hutchins, stating in a footnote concerning Mary's case that 'Tradition reports, that there was a woman burnt in the same place, [Maumbury Rings] for the same crime, 100 years before.'

Mary's parents were clearly financially feeling the pinch of supporting her in gaol. They must have laid out a considerable amount in the pursuance of a pardon for their daughter – in their desperation they may even have resorted to bribes. As a consequence, 'for want of the usual pay' Mary was removed by Mr Knapton, the Governor of the town gaol (who later became Mayor of Dorchester in 1713) from her 'convenient chamber' down to the common room for condemned women. Mary no longer presented the lucrative prospect of being a *milch-kine* (milk cow), an old slang term used by gaolers for 'when their prisoners will bleed freely [i.e. to part with their money easily] to have some Favour'. Now, as a prisoner without means, she was lodged in an overcrowded lice-ridden chamber, the brutal and unsanitary conditions of which meant that the probability of death by disease or starvation was a very real one which would likely claim many sharing her confinement before their term of imprisonment was up or death sentence could be enacted.

In these reduced circumstances, Mary's parents appear to have been unable to provide their daughter with even the basic comfort of a bed (even though the authorities assured them that this would be returned after her execution!) which would have been welcome, not least in view of the fact that Mary was now in the advanced stages of pregnancy. The best that could be managed was the provision of a bed improvised from the canvas tilting of an old wagon, a 'tilt' being the awning-like structure on a covered wagon. It was in these spartan conditions that on Wednesday, 19 December Mary delivered a son – and given the circumstances of his birth, this was surely a 'Wednesday's child full of woe'. In all likelihood, in view of the Brookes' family's depleted finances, the prospect of a midwife attending the birth is doubtful, so Mary was reliant on the support of her mother and possibly some other woman experienced in assisting in childbirth drawn from the ranks of the females incarcerated along with her in Dorchester gaol; perhaps it may even have been the gaoler's wife. The infant, whose name we do not know – this was deliberately not given in the *Serious Admonitions to Youth* to protect his identity – was baptised immediately at Mary's request. Though there is no record of a baptism in the transcription of the register of All Saints Church for the period where it would should have appeared, as the gaol fell within this parish, had the baptism been recorded, it would have been intriguing to note the paternity entered in the register, though doubtless it would have stated 'Father: Thomas Channing', for form's sake, even if Mary had been confident to the contrary. Whether or not Mary herself was still adherent to the Anabaptist faith in which she had been raised, advocating the delay of baptism until adulthood, the conditions in which Mary had given birth in all likelihood prompted the hasty christening of the baby, the prospect of the prevalent high infant mortality rate doubtless exacerbated by a prison birth.

Once the child was born, Mary's father, fearing the expedition of her execution, renewed his efforts to obtain a pardon, this time, petition in hand, waylaying the Queen herself as she came out of chapel, but again his efforts were to no avail. We know from the Declared Accounts in the *Calendar for Treasury Books* that in December 1705, Queen Anne was resident at St James's Palace, therefore, Richard Brookes must have travelled to London and intercepted her as she exited the Chapel Royal; located within the main block of the Palace. He must have been very determined to get that far and waylay the monarch in person and must have known it was his last chance. Now despairing of ever being able to save his daughter, Richard Brookes 'contented himself with frequent addresses to the Almighty, for the good of her soul.'

Those entreaties of her father on the part of Mary's soul might well have proved timely as during her lying-in, an old practice involving a woman having a period of bed rest after giving birth which traditionally lasted a month to allow her to regain her strength, Mary succumbed to a violent fever, undoubtedly as a consequence of childbirth in such squalid conditions. In all probability, she was suffering from puerperal fever, or 'childbed' fever, then a common postpartum infection contracted following childbirth and a significant cause of maternal mortality in the eighteenth century. Though the term puerperal fever could be applied to any fever arising in consequence of pregnancy or delivery and occurring during the lying-in period, nevertheless such infections were estimated to have accounted for half of all maternal deaths. Because many of the causative organisms of postpartum infections were already present in the environment, women were often resistant to them and only succumbed if they sustained excessive trauma during the birth, or from problems such as a retained placenta, so in all probability Mary had endured a difficult delivery, or wanted for experienced care afterwards, on top of to having to give birth in less than ideal surroundings. The death of Mary Wollstonecraft, the English writer, philosopher and advocate of women's rights, was a classic case of puerperal fever contracted as a consequence of a retained placenta; though the birth of her first and only child went smoothly, the placenta did not follow. The midwife attending her panicked and a doctor was called, who opted to tear out the placenta himself by reaching inside his patient. As the sepsis inevitably spread through Wollstonecraft's body, she died eleven days after the birth on 10 September 1797. Mary's condition must have been further exacerbated however by her mother's insistence that the baby should not be taken from her, her insistence that Mary continue to nurse the newborn further weakening her constitution; Mary must still have been a fighter nevertheless, as she survived. Though Mrs Brookes remained by her daughter's side constantly, why she refused to allow the child to be removed from Dorchester gaol is a mystery – especially considering her daughter's precarious state of health. In view of the child's doubtful paternity, Elizabeth Brookes was unlikely to have been driven by concerns that the Channing family would have taken custody of the baby and while we do not know if the child even survived, if he did thrive, the most likely eventuality is that he was taken care of and raised by the Brookes family anyway.

Whatever the reason, as the Lent assize for Dorchester came around again, on Friday, 8 March 1706, in a pitiful state, the emaciated Mary was again summoned to the bar and asked if she could show just reason why the former sentence handed down to her last July should not be passed. She could not. Physically and mentally depleted, her appearance must have visibly shocked those in the courtroom. She said nothing other than maintaining her innocence of the crime for which she had been found guilty, saying that she was 'as innocent as the child unborn'. However on being told that this was not a sufficient plea, she was ordered to prepare for death; the sentence had merely been deferred – in law, she was already dead.

When Mary returned to Dorchester gaol, she took one of the other women prisoners by the hand and, with some earnestness, told her that 'twas with great joy she received the news of meeting the Lord'. Though she was obviously resigned to her fate and knew that her time was running short, in spite of the entreaties of the Reverend Hutchins and several other clergymen of the town, Mary still refused to confess to the crime for which she was to die. Yet at this time she asked for herself to be baptised. Unconvinced of her sincere repentance, the Reverend Hutchins initially refused Mary's request. However in such a weighty spiritual matter, deciding not to place reliance on his judgement alone, Hutchins consulted other brethren in the local clergy. Yet their opinions remained divided, so direction from the Bishop of Bristol, in whose diocese Dorchester fell, was sought. In turn, his Lordship, feeling that as he was absent from the situation and not best able to judge himself, gave the power of decision to Hutchins, directing him to 'do as he thought convenient'. After again seeking the advice of several neighbouring clergymen, Hutchins relented and the baptism of Mary Channing went ahead on Sunday, 17 March, though again, as with the baptism of her son, there is no trace of a baptismal record for Mary in the transcription of the registers of All Saints Church, Dorchester. Now that she had been formally received into the Church of England, with the date set for Mary's execution the following Thursday, 21 March, the Reverend Hutchins had only four days left in which to persuade a confession from the most recently admitted member of his flock.

For her part, Mary appeared 'uneasy and displeased' whenever the subject of her guilt was raised, yet when told that confessing to God alone would assure 'her the object of His mercy' she seemed comforted. Perhaps Mary then had made her own peace with her Maker. Present night and day until the eve of her daughter's execution, Elizabeth Brookes was derided for blaming the judicial system for her daughter's plight and indeed for backing Mary's persistent refusal to a confession, which in the view of the established church effectively damned her soul. The *Serious Admonition to Youth* noted early on that Mary's childhood was one 'not illuminated with the Rising Sun of Religious Inclinations and Actions', but in support of Elizabeth Brookes' stance, if she honestly believed in her daughter's innocence, then she also fervently believed that a false confession on Mary's part, to appease the Reverend Hutchins, or any other clergymen not of the Anabaptist sect, would carry no weight. With regards to Mary's own request for orthodox Christian baptism, as she appears herself to have shown scant devotion to *any* religion during her lifetime, this request, so late in the day, may have been no more than a ploy to convince the Reverend Hutchins that she was open to religious conformity, she perhaps desperately hoping that this might reinforce her optimistic confidence in a last minute acquittal, if she maintained her protestations of innocence. Indeed, prior to her execution several clergymen who were with her in Dorchester gaol noted that Mary was:

'upon her guard when any questions were asked relating to the fact [of her guilt], and her wariness in answering, gave several persons reason to believe, that she had, even to the last, great hopes of saving her life, by a positive denial.'

Whether or not she was in fact innocent, she was to remain steadfast to her denial, even up until the moment she was tied to the stake.

Chapter 7

'And that dismal day being now come'

As dawn broke on the morning of the day set for Mary's execution, Thursday, 21 March, perhaps she had lain awake all night in her cell, or maybe she awoke only to be jolted from hopeful dreams of deliverance; we can assume that her baby was still with her. Though Elizabeth Brookes had insisted that the child remain with Mary, in spite of the detrimental and weakening effects that continued nursing had had on her poor state of health, at the time it was nevertheless common practice for a woman's children to accompany their mother to prison and remain there with her, especially in the case of infants classed as care-dependent of a nursing mother. Of course, the heart-wrenching eventuality of this practice meant that children often remained in the cell with their mother up until the time they were taken for execution, clinging on for dear life as their parent was led away to the gallows, or the stake, as in Mary's case. Presumably as the time neared, Mrs Brookes would have taken the baby, who, at just thirteen weeks old was mercifully unaware of the circumstances of his removal from his mother's arms. What anguish must Mary have suffered?

Later that morning, Mary may well have heard the preparations for the removal of the two other condemned prisoners whose executions were to proceed hers. Though Gallows Hill, on the junction of Icen Way and South Walks was the main site for public executions in Dorchester, at some point, around the year 1700, public executions were moved to a gallows sited at Maumbury Rings. Prior to the executions held within the ancient Roman Amphitheatre, however, countless condemned men, women and children would have made their last journey along Gaol Lane, now Icen Way, the final section leading to Gallows Hill. Said to still echo with the sounds of ghostly cries, along this narrow lane, further constricted by the obligatory jeering crowds, in the past heretics had been dragged by their heels, tied to horses frightened by the taunting howls of the mob, to be strung up and disemboweled while still alive on the spot now marked by the Dorset Martyrs' Memorial. Created by Dame Elisabeth Frink and erected in 1986, the larger than life bronze statues of two martyrs facing a representation of Death commemorates the countless men and women – both Catholic and

Protestant – who were executed for their adherence to their faith during the religious troubles of the sixteenth and seventeenth centuries, one of whom was the Catholic chaplain, Hugh Green, mentioned in the first chapter, after whose execution the mob played football with his head. Anti-Catholic feeling throughout the country again ran high in 1850, when the Pope instructed Cardinal Wiseman to restore the Catholic hierarchy in England; Dorchester's Maumbury Rings were again the venue for a baying crowd when on 5 November that year – Guy Fawkes Night – a demonstration was held during which a torchlit procession culminated in the burning of effigies of the Pope and Wiseman, witnessed by the then 10-year-old Thomas Hardy, taken there by his father, who though he had scant understanding of the proceedings, nevertheless found the whole episode grimly exciting, but was also perplexed by the appearance of one of the 'evil monks' in the procession who bore a marked resemblance to a man who worked for his father!

Though now defunct, the Gallows Hill execution apparatus, as shown on John Speed's plan of Dorchester dating to 1610, was made up of two uprights and a crossbeam connecting them with enough space for a two-wheeled cart to pass through, with enough space for multiple hangings. This was the design repeated for the gallows set up in the former gladiatorial amphitheatre, as shown in the 1755 engraving featured in *Grose's Antiquities of England and Wales*. The illustration shows the gallows standing on the west side of the amphitheatre, between the monumental earthworks and the Weymouth Road. Before this engraving of the Maumbury gallows had been executed (no pun intended!) the antiquarian and pioneering archaeologist William Stukeley, who was later to survey Stonehenge and was the first to record the Avenue and the nearby Cursus, wrote in 1723 in his *Of the Roman Amphitheatre at Dorchester* that:

> 'the amphitheatre was in greater perfection before the gallows was removed hither by an unlucky humour of the Sheriff; since when the parapet at top is on that side much beaten down by the trampling of men and horses at executions.'

Stukeley alludes to the further damage wrought to the ancient site by the siting of the gallows there: 'the parapet is now 3 or 4 foot high; but much ruined on that side next the gallows, since last year at an execution'. However, we know that Mary's execution took place on the floor of the amphitheatre in 1706, though had the old Gallows Hill site still been in operation she would have met her end there. In fact, the gallows at Maumbury would seem to have been in regular use up to the time that the new prison was built, completed in the year 1795, so, while there is a suggestion that executions also took place at the gibbet which had been set up in 1767 on the Bridport Road at Bradford Down about a mile and a half outside of Dorchester, in all likelihood the gibbet here was only used for the display of the bodies of executed criminals, intended as a deterrent to would-be lawbreakers. Between the Summer Assizes of 1736 and the Lent Assize of 1795 it is recorded that forty-four felons were executed at Maumbury Rings, before public executions were moved to an area outside the new gaol, by which time the more humane method of dispatching prisoners was employed, their death hastened by hanging them from a 'longer drop', the method designed to break the prisoner's neck by allowing them to fall a predetermined distance and then be brought up with a sharp jerk by the rope. Prior to this, the type of gallows used was the 'short drop', resulting in death by strangulation, which could take several minutes before the victim lost consciousness. Preserved in Dorset County Museum are a pair of lead weights engraved with the word 'MERCY', provided by the then altruistic governor of Dorchester Gaol to hasten the end of Silvester Wilkins, a very light subject, executed in 1833 for arson at Bridport.

Returning to Mary's final hours, at about noon on the 21st, the two other prisoners condemned to death that day, both men, were hanged on the amphitheatre gallows. Presumably, both had been found guilty at the Dorchester Lent assizes held the fortnight previously, the same court before which Mary had appeared again to receive the reinstatement of her sentence after the birth of her child. Of the two men who had gone ahead of her, one had received the death sentence for housebreaking, while the other prisoner on the gallows that afternoon had been convicted for the murder of his wife, who, though he 'shewed not the least care for his soul, but died and ignorant, hardened wretch', nevertheless protested his innocence, 'denying to the very last the fact for which he suffer'd'.

We can assume that at the time of the noon executions the headcount was already mounting within the Rings, the numbers growing in anticipation of the day's 'main event' as public executions, or 'hanging fairs' as they were known, always attracted large crowds. Although the public spectacle of execution was supposed to act as a deterrent to the populace, making them afraid of falling victim to the same fate, this was clearly not the case. The barbaric spectacle of public execution was thought by the authorities to be morally improving to society at large; however, quite the opposite was true. Amongst the crowds, which were often numbering in the thousands, were those who drank too much, the rowdier contingent degenerating into a drunken rabble who would shout, curse and jeer at those unfortunates who were about to be hanged, or 'turned-off' to use the terminology of the age. To quote Dr Johnson's opinion of public execution: 'If they do not draw spectators, they do not answer their purpose'; but he had clearly missed the point, as public executions often took on a mass entertainment quality, perhaps akin to an open-air concert atmosphere today. Human nature being what it is, these events turned out to be a perversely enjoyable distraction from the routine grind of everyday life. With food and drink on sale and souvenirs being hawked, crowds including families with young children would bring along a picnic and make a day of it, whilst in the midst of those laughing and joking about the awful sight they were about to witness, pickpockets and tricksters exploited the opportunity to work the crowd, literally in the shadow of the gallows. Despite the undeniable taste and enthusiasm for the spectacle of a public execution being an obvious draw, the anticipation would have been heightened on that Thursday afternoon by the prospect of a public burning. Indeed, Maumbury Rings was an excellent venue with regards to staging – as the former amphitheatre presented an arena with tiers of seats on all sides, not only was everyone assured a good view, as was intended in Roman times, but the arrangement also meant that the problems presented by crowd-control were easier to deal with. And, according to John Hutchins in *The History and Antiquities of the County of Dorset*, there were as many as 10,000 spectators who filled the sides and top of the arena on that day, on the floor of which the stake and piled faggots (bundles of dry brushwood) had been prepared for Mary. From the centre of the Rings, the solitary 19-year-old girl would face the multitude come to witness her public strangulation and burning.

Perhaps we should take a moment here to revisit the barbaric death sentence imposed for those found guilty of petty treason – the penalty for which Mary was to suffer as she was found guilty of the murder of her husband. As outlined in the introduction, Petty Treason or *petit treason* was an offence under the common law of England which involved the betrayal (including murder) of a superior by a subordinate. It differed from the better known offence of High Treason in that this was a crime that was, and still can, only be committed against the sovereign. It was not until the *Offences against the Person Act* passed in 1828 that in England and Wales Petty Treason ceased to be a distinct offence from murder. It was abolished in Ireland in 1829 and it had never existed in Scotland. Prior to this reforming legislation, it was the element of betrayal which marked Petty Treason out as a crime more heinous than that of ordinary murder. Stemming from the medieval and post-medieval societal hierarchy in which each person had his or her appointed place, such murders were seen as threatening to the status quo – those holding a superior place in society feared the consequences if murder by their subordinates was not harshly punished. As an aggravated form of murder, Petty Treason was codified early on as a common law offence under the Treason Act of 1351, and as such was applicable to a wife killing her husband, a clergyman killing his prelate (a high-ranking member of the clergy) or a servant killing his master or mistress, or his master's wife. There were three other forms of Petty Treason which had existed under common law before being abolished by the above act, and these included a wife just *attempting* to kill her husband, a servant forging his master's seal, or a servant committing adultery with his master's wife or daughter. While the vast majority of cases of Petty Treason tried in the eighteenth century involved women who had murdered their husbands, a number of servants (both male and female) were indicted for killing their employers. Counterfeiting gold or silver coin was also classed as the crime of Petty Treason, that is until the 1351 Act elevated this offence to that of High Treason. The offence of 'coining' covered several individual offences relating only to gold and silver coins, e.g. clipping coins to provide coin metal for forgeries, colouring coins to make them appear of higher value, making counterfeit coins and having the equipment to do any of the above. Coining was considered treasonable because it was a crime of disloyalty to the Crown, directly affecting the State and confidence in the currency.

However, the methods and the inequality of modes of execution remained unchanged. The punishment for a man convicted of Petty Treason was almost the same as for a normal felony execution, that is, hanging, but with the added shame and discomfort of being 'drawn' to the place of execution, seated backwards on a wattle sledge or hurdle, drawn behind a horse, rather than the customary ride of the condemned man in a cart. A man executed for Petty Treason would not however be 'quartered' as this punishment was reserved for cases of High Treason, 'quartering' occurring after the condemned was hanged, almost to the point of death, then emasculated, disembowelled, beheaded and quartered, that is, chopped into four pieces, their remains often displayed in prominent places across the country as a warning to others who might think to attack the monarch's authority. By contrast, the punishment for a woman convicted of Petty Treason was virtually the same as if they had committed High Treason – that she be burned at the stake – though she would not be 'drawn' to the place of execution as this was reserved for those women found guilty of High Treason. In some parts of continental Europe, those who murdered their husbands could be executed by drowning as well as being burned alive. The basis for this disparity in punishments stemmed from a concern for public sensibility, summed up in Judge Blackstone's commentaries, his explanation for the differing punishment given to women for the crime of High Treason being that 'the decency due to the sex forbids the exposing and publicly mangling their bodies and their sentence is, to be drawn to the gallows and there be burnt alive'. Though the question of public decency was clearly the impetus for the burning of women in cases of High Treason, the same punishment was nevertheless enacted for the lesser crime of Petty Treason and still carried out over a century after the punishment was last invoked in a case of High Treason. Elizabeth Gaunt was the last woman to be burnt for High Treason. She was executed in 1685, having been convicted of involvement in the Rye House plot, an abortive anti-Catholic plan to assassinate King Charles II and his brother James, Duke of York.

While the horrific punishment of burning at the stake remains in the popular imagination as one reserved for witches and heretics, who were indeed consigned to the 'purifying' flames while still alive, the law did latterly offer a modicum of mercy to women found guilty of either count of treason, allowing for the executioner to render them 'senseless' before the fire took hold. Equipped with a cord, the executioner would pass it around the prisoner's throat, standing outside of the fire. He would then pull it tight so that the victim would be effectively strangled before the flames could reach her. Before the adoption of this practice, however, it was not unknown for women about to be burned to be draped in cloth or dressed in clothes that had been impregnated with tar, the idea being that this would speed their agonising death. Eleanor Elsam, who was burned at Lincoln in 1722, had her legs, feet and arms tarred before she was consigned to the flames and was even wearing a tarred bonnet – and we can only hope that her suffering was over before the fire reached her flammable headgear – a parallel perhaps to the bags of gunpowder tied between the legs and under each arm, or strung about the necks of heretics in order to hasten their end as the flames rose. Those heretics 'lucky' enough to have well-stoked fires would soon have met an explosive end, while others not so fortunate suffered longer as a consequence of 'green' wood or a strong wind blowing in the wrong direction.

With regards to the practice of prior strangulation, this seems to have become increasingly the norm in the latter part of the seventeenth century, taking as an example the execution of Ann Evans who, in 1675, was burned in Plymouth for committing petty treason; after mounting a box and being fastened to the stake by her neck, she was surrounded with kindling, at which point:

> '... the hangman would have set fire unto the furze before she was strangled but some more charitable and tender-hearted, cryed [sic] to him to take away the Block from under her Feet; which having done, she soon fell down, and expired in a Trice'.

Similarly, at the execution of Esther Ives, having been found guilty at the Winchester assize of 1686 of assisting her lover to strangle her husband (I will refrain from pointing out the irony here) it was recorded that '... after the executioner had strangled her, the fire was kindled'. In a few instances, however, the timing and differing methods of this merciful procedure could go awry, with the cord burning through or the victim regaining consciousness, being consequently burned alive.

One such instance occurred in 1726, when Catherine Hayes went to the stake for spousal homicide, though this particular 'hanging day' seems to have been fraught with many problems. This mother of twelve children was condemned after having connived with her lovers, two men named Wood and Billings who lodged with the couple, to kill her husband, John Hayes. On 1 March 1726, after getting Hayes drunk, they killed him, disposing of the corpse by flinging a trunk full of cut up body parts into a pond at Marylebone Fields. Yet the mistake which led to their discovery was the casting of Hayes' severed head in a bucket into the Thames, as it was washed up on the following tide. Displayed in the churchyard of St Margaret's, Westminster, for several days until it was identified, the guilty parties were soon apprehended. Wood died in Newgate before the day set for the murderous trio's execution. Catherine herself tried to escape her fate but was unsuccessful in attempting to poison herself. Consequently, on 9 May, while Billings, charged with murder, was hanged, Catherine Hayes accordingly suffered the penalty for Petty Treason. Catherine would have been led past the lifeless body of Billings who had already been executed, burnings ordinarily beginning several minutes after the other condemned prisoners had been hanged, with prisoners led past the bodies suspended at the gallows on their way to the stake. On that day, two other prisoners had already attempted to escape from the carts carrying them to execution, having freed themselves from their nooses and wrist ties. As if this was not excitement enough, then one of the spectators' grandstands collapsed, killing at least two people and injuring several more. Finally, Catherine's execution was horribly botched. Literally burned to death, the executioner having lost his grip on the rope with which he intended to strangle her, the *Newgate Calendar*, that hugely popular monthly bulletin, yet a supposedly moralising publication that gave vivid accounts of notorious criminals in the eighteenth and nineteenth centuries, reported that:

'... the spectators behind her pushing the faggots from her, while she rent the air with her cries and lamentations. Other faggots were instantly thrown on her; but she survived amidst the flames for a considerable time, and her body was not perfectly reduced to ashes in less than three hours ...'

A later account however stated that:

'... the executioner was foiled in an endeavour to strangle her by the burning of the rope, and the woman was finally killed by a piece of wood which was thrown at her head and dashed out her brains.'

Either way, this was a nightmarish end.

Such executions by burning continued until almost into the nineteenth century, yet with one meagre nod toward public decency, as from the 1780s, the bodies of strangled women were usually completely covered with faggots prior to the fire being lit. Eventually, the voices of those with influence and who were strongly critical of this form of punishment, augmented by public outcry, as well as the ensuing scandals of mismanaged executions, brought about the abolition of this punishment and its substitution by hanging. An article in *The Times* newspaper which appeared after the execution of Margaret Sullivan on 25 June 1788 ran:

'There is something inhuman in burning a woman, for what only subjects a man to hanging. Human nature should shudder at the idea.'

It was Christian Murphy who was the last woman to be officially burned at the stake in England. As mentioned in the previous chapter, on failing to 'plead her belly' after being found guilty of High Treason as a 'coiner', she was executed on the morning of 18 March 1789 outside Newgate prison 'drest in a clean striped gown, a white ribbon, and a black ribbon round her cap', and though her execution received virtually no attention from the newspapers (perhaps owing to practical limitations at the time on how much news they could publish across only four pages) her fate served to as the incentive and motivation behind Sir Benjamin Hammett's introduction to Parliament of a Bill for Altering the Sentence of Burning Women the following year. A former sheriff of London, Hammett was also an MP, strongly opposed to the punishment, denouncing is as 'the savage remains of Norman policy' which 'disgraced our statutes, as 'the practice did the common law'. Hammett's bill was introduced just in time to save 25-year-old Sophia Girton from the fire, just four days prior to the day set for her burning. Convicted of coining at the Old Bailey on 24 April 1790, Sophia was in fact pardoned on condition of transportation for life to New South Wales. Yet so many, like Mary Channing, had suffered before her.

On the day of Mary's execution, while the prior hanging of the two condemned men had taken place at around noon, it was 5 o'clock before Mary's time came, the proceedings delayed while the under-sheriff enjoyed his tea. Each county had a High Sheriff who was appointed for a year and had the responsibility, amongst other things, of carrying out the punishments ordered by the courts. In capital cases, it was the sheriff's responsibility to organise the execution and appoint the executioner from an approved list, although this was usually delegated to an Under Sheriff, as in this instance, who, incredibly, delayed Mary's execution until after he had eaten. He had to be present at the execution and also had to pay the hangman (whose remit would have included the strangulation of Mary at the stake) and his assistant(s), then claim the money back through 'sheriff's cravings' from the Home Office. The execution would proceed under the direction of the sheriff and went ahead irrespective of whether there might be the possibility of a reprieve, even at the last minute.

It might be pertinent here, in view of Thomas Hardy's particular interest in Mary, some would say an obsession, in view of his enduring fascination with the details of her case, which had preoccupied him since a much earlier stage in his life, to let him pick up the story with an extract from the article commissioned by *The Times* Newspaper, appearing on 9 October 1908. Mary's fate included in the piece, prompted after recent archaeological excavations had revealed that Maumbury was originally a Neolithic hill-top henge, extensively adapted by the Romans for use as an amphitheatre. Hardy wrote:

'On that day two men were hanged before her turn came, and then, "the under sheriff having taken some refreshment," he proceeded to his biggest and last job with this girl not yet 19, now reduced to a skeleton by the long fever, and already more dead than alive. She was conveyed from the gaol in a cart by her father and husbands houses so the course of the procession must have been up High-East Street as far as the Bow [the junction where South and High East streets join, two houses once stood, close together and with rooms projecting over the street, making for a narrow and inconvenient passage and consequently pulled down in 1748] thence down South Street and up the straight Roman Road to the Ring beside it.'

After arriving at Maumbury Rings, the Reverend Hutchins and other clergymen continued for some time in prayer with Mary and again, though she was pressed for a confession, none was forthcoming, though it was noted that in the midst of her prayers Mary was 'strangely concerned' on seeing one face in the crowd – that of Richard Channing, her husband's eldest brother, and it was with 'some difficulty that Mr. Hutchins brought her again to a calm Attendance on her Devotions.'

Hardy's article picks up again here:

'When fixed to the stake she justified her innocence to the very last, and left the world with a courage seldom found in her sex. She being first strangled, the fire was kindled about five in the afternoon, and in the sight of many thousands she was consumed to ashes.'

Hardy's article went on to elaborate over the barbarity and horrific circumstances of Mary's execution, still difficult to stomach today:

'There is nothing to show she was dead before the burning began, and from the use of the word "strangled" and not "hanged" it would seem that she was merely rendered insensible before the fire was lit. An ancestor of the present writer, who witnessed the scene, has handed down the information that "her heart leapt out" during the burning, and other curious details that cannot be printed here. Was man ever slaughtered by his fellow man during the Roman or barbarian use of this place of games or of sacrifice in circumstances of greater atrocity?'

Clearly, Hardy did not feel that he could impart all that had been 'handed down' in his article however, perhaps with a view to offending the sensibilities of *The Times'* readership, he omitting certain details recorded in his 'Personal Notebooks', in particularly those from the entry made on 25 January 1919, which ran:

> 'Mr Prideaux tells me more details of the death of Mary Channing (burnt for the poisoning of her husband [not proven]) in 1705, [OS] in Maumbury Ring, Dorchester. They were told him by old Mr. ---, a direct descendant of one who was a witness of the execution. He said that after she had been strangled & the burning had commenced, she recovered consciousness [owing to the pain from the flames probably] & writhed and shrieked. One of the constables thrust a swab into her mouth to stop her cries, & the milk from her bosoms (she had lately given birth to a child) squirted out into their faces "and made 'em jump back."'

Whatever its basis in truth, this is a brutal account and one that is certainly disquieting to imagine. Indeed the effect of this horrific spectacle must have had a lasting impact on the ghoulish crowds come to witness Mary's execution that day, clearly getting more of a spectacle than they bargained for, Hardy further recording from his informant's account that '... with other details handed down from my respected ancestor who was present (such as the smell of roa[s]t meat, &c.) gives sufficiently horrible picture', this gruesome aspect alluded to by Hardy when referencing Mary's story in Chapter XI of *The Mayor of Casterbridge* : '... that not one of those ten thousand people ever cared particularly for hot roast after that.'

For Mary now at last the suffering was over. It was not recorded how long it took for the flames to entirely consume her body; neither were the weather conditions reported on that day, so whether or not a stiff March breeze was blowing it may have taken some time. As mentioned earlier, the body of Catherine Hayes 'was not perfectly reduced to ashes until three hours later'. As the multitude dispersed, the faces and clothes of the ones who had been on the wrong side of the fire possibly grey with wood-ash, and their collective stomachs presumably turned by the inhalation of the pall of human smoke, their sheer numbers would have choked the streets and their passage would have been slow, either to their homes – though possibly not relishing the thought of supper – or to the tavern to discuss the day's events. Whether Mary's ashes were blown away on the wind, or gathered up and given burial by her nearest and dearest we do not know. The disposal of ashes by scattering into flowing water was generally reserved for those burned for heresy. It was sometimes the case that any remaining ashes or surviving fragments of bone identifiable as human, which would be very few, if any, would be gathered and afterwards buried. Indeed, Elizabeth Boardingham, the last woman to be burned at York in 1776, while awaiting execution with her lover, Thomas Aikney, had asked that her charred remains be buried along with him, though the sentiment may have been one-sided on Elizabeth's part, some observers claiming that she shook Aikney's hand as they parted at York's Tyburn, Elizabeth having asked him for a kiss, which Aikney refused.

After the execution, presumably all the parties involved tried to pick up their lives in and around Dorchester as best they could. As hypothesised earlier, Mary's baby was in all probability taken into the Brookes household to be raised – what became of the boy we will never know, whether he grew up in the shadow cast by the shame of his mother's conviction and whether it was even warranted – certainly there were doubts in Thomas Hardy's mind, who said that he had:

> 'examined more than once a report of her trial, and can find no distinct evidence that the thoughtless, pleasure-loving creature committed the crime, while it contains much to suggest that she did not'.

As for the Channings, from their point of view, justice had now been served upon the woman who was the means of depriving them of their Thomas and to them it had probably seemed a long time coming – after all Thomas Channing's body had been laid to rest near on a year prior to his wife's execution. After Thomas's death, as soon as the Coroner's inquest had been held, following the autopsy carried out at the behest of his father, his remains had been transferred to Maiden Newton, from where the family hailed, for burial amongst his ancestors. It was noted that on 24 April 1705, Thomas' funeral procession through the village to St Mary's Church was accompanied by sixty to eighty people on horseback, Thomas and the Channing family at large being so well respected in the district.

Though time must have done something to dull the collective censure of the Brookes family, the folklore and tales that were the upshot of Mary's fate nevertheless guaranteed a lasting memory, and one which was to which prove the inspiration, and it must be said an enduring source of fascination, for one of the most renowned poets and novelists in English literary history, and necessarily why the next chapter is devoted to the insights of Thomas Hardy.

Chapter 8

Hardy's Inspiration

Few writer's works are as suffused with their native landscape as Thomas Hardy's novels and poetry, and figuring large in the landscape of his mind, many of Hardy's settings are inseparable from the places that inspired them. Indeed, much of his appeal lies in his abstractions of Wessex, his revival of the ancient Saxon name for the southwestern counties of England which he described as 'a partly-real, partly dream-country'. *Far from the Madding Crowd* (1874), introduced the Wessex area setting. In the last edition of that novel, Hardy reminds himself and his readers that it was in its pages that he first made use of the ancient name of Wessex, described as 'a merely realistic dream country' and the backdrop for all his major novels. And it was Hardy's and Mary Channing's home town of Dorchester that was the basis for the Casterbridge of his tales, the town itself figuring as prominently as the characters in his writing, an affirmation of which is the blue plaque affixed to the flint-faced building on South Street, currently a Barclay's Bank, proudly proclaiming, 'This house is reputed to have been lived in by the Mayor of Casterbridge'. Absorbed as he was with the history, fabric and features of the town, what would have been Hardy's impression of the statue of himself unveiled just three years after his death? Occupying pride of place at the top of the High Street that the author knew so well, one of the most recognisable landmarks in Dorset's county town, a thoughtful looking bronze, Hardy is depicted sitting on a tree stump with a book in his lap ;it is said that the decision to sculpt Hardy seated was taken to compensate for the fact that he was known to be very short in stature! Nevertheless, the statue is a testament to the impact that Hardy has had on the town and the recognisable inspirations which he drew that were and are instrumental in shaping the conceptions of Dorchester, and its inhabitants, to this day.

While of course, the story of Dorchester's own Mary Channing was the impetus for *The Mock Wife*, and as mentioned in the previous chapter, her execution was also referenced in *The Mayor of Casterbridge*, other aspects of Dorchester's past, real and imagined, were influential on Hardy, as well as incidents he experienced during his own lifetime; though renamed,

Dorchester was always more than recognisable in his work. While this chapter is primarily concerned the exploration of Mary Channing as the focus of Hardy's Dorchester inspirations, in view of his misgivings over her guilt, and indeed his concern with the plight and position of women at large, other of the enormous influences on his work from Dorchester are necessarily included; those who were a victim of circumstance were after all a recurring theme throughout Hardy's work.

Hardy was born in Higher Bockhampton, a small village just three miles outside Dorchester, in 1840. The eldest son of Thomas Hardy and Jemima (née Hand), the couple's unplanned pregnancy having forced their marriage toward the end of 1839, his father was a stonemason and builder; but it was his mother who passed on her love of reading and books to her son. Hardy's childhood was a somewhat isolated existence, though self-imposed, his formative years marked by his fascination with and exploration of the open countryside surrounding his home, the experiences of rural life in his formative years figuring prominently in many of his novels, and while one reviewer described how 'the sweet and liberal air of Dorset blows through' Hardy's second published novel, *Under the Greenwood Tree* (1872), his depictions of 'rough frank life' and his tragic characters struggling against their passions and social circumstances in a declining rural society felt real enough. Hardy's Wessex was one that he neither idealised or romanticised.

When he was eight years old, Hardy went to a local school in Dorchester, walking the three miles each way in all weathers, tramping down country lanes and traversing fields, crossing the water meadows between Grey's Bridge and Swan Bridge until he reached the edge of the town, the paved, steeply rising High Street with its old churches, newly built town hall and busy shops and inns a far cry from the hamlet that was his home. He received only a modest education which lasted until he was sixteen; though he had wanted to attend university and become an Anglican minister, the Hardy family's finances would not allow for this ambition and besides, his declining interest in religion swayed Hardy away from that vocation and more toward that of self-study of poetry and writing. So in 1856 Hardy, just after his sixteenth birthday, started working for John Hicks, a local architect whose offices were at 39 South Street, Dorchester. It was while he was apprenticed to Hicks that he witnessed the execution of Elizabeth Martha Brown and, in parallel to Mary Channing's fate as the last woman burned at the stake in Dorset, Brown's execution was to be the last public hanging of a woman in Dorset.

Acknowledged as the inspiration for Hardy's novel *Tess of the D'Urbervilles*, Martha Brown was executed outside Dorchester Gaol on Saturday, 9 of

August 1856 after being convicted of the murder of her second husband, John Brown, on 22 July, just thirteen days earlier. Among the four thousand strong crowd who thronged to watch the hanging was Thomas Hardy. When he was a child, Hardy had been affected by a story told him by his father, which must have dated back to the times of troubled rural unrest in the 1830s, when Thomas Hardy senior had witnessed four men hanged outside Dorchester prison for simply being in the company of some others who had set fire to a hay rick. One of their number was a half-starved boy who had merely run up to see the blaze, but was convicted with the others none-theless and when it came to his execution, as he was of such slight build, weights were affixed to his feet ensuring that when the drop fell his neck would break and hasten his end. Presumably this was Silvester Wilkins, the same unfortunate mentioned in the previous chapter, executed in 1833 for arson and for whom the 'Mercy weights' were provided, still in the collection of the Dorset County Museum. Childhood stories aside, witnessing the spectacle of Martha Brown's execution in person clearly made an indelible impression on the teenage Hardy, as he was to write seventy years later that he was 'ashamed' to have been present, 'my only excuse being that I was but a youth, and had to be in town at that time for other reasons ...' Clearly the shame came later, as on that day, Hardy, who was accompanied by a friend, managed to secure a good vantage point in a tree very close to the gallows, erected the evening before over the gateway of the new entrance leading to Dorset County Gaol from North Square, on what became the former prison car park.

Yet it was not merely the execution itself which had such a lasting impression on Hardy, as much as the other finer details of the day. On that morning a few minutes after 8 o'clock, Martha Brown, dressed in the long, tight fitting thin black silk dress, which she had chosen to wear for hanging, after shaking hands with the prison officials began to ascend to the scaffold. After climbing the first flight of eleven steps, the forbidding figure of the hangman, William Calcraft, stood waiting to pinion her arms in front of her before leading her up the next flight of nineteen steps, across a platform and on up the last flight of steps to the actual drop. Here Calcraft, who was noted for his 'short drops', causing most of his victims to die a slow and ago-nising death, put a white hood over her head and the simple noose around her neck. Proceeding to go down below the trap to withdraw the bolts (there was no lever in those days), it was pointed out to him that he had not pin-ioned Martha's legs. In accordance with the Victorian preoccupation with decency, Calcraft returned and put a strap around Martha's legs, outside of her dress, to prevent it billowing up and exposing her legs as she dropped. While the proper forms were observed, Martha stood stoically on the gallows, supported by a male warder on each side, calmly awaiting her death. As it was a drizzly morning, the rain made the hood covering Martha's head damp, and it clung to her face. Hardy recalled, 'I saw—they had put a cloth over the face—how, as the cloth got wet, *her features came through it*. That was extraordinary.' When the end came, the *Reading Mercury* of 16 August 1856, reported that '...the wretched woman fell with great force, and after a few struggles ceased to exist.' Hardy's macabre captivation with the post-execution scene prompted his further, some have intimated questionable, recollection:

> 'I remember what a fine figure she showed against the sky as she hung in the misty rain and how the tight black silk gown set off her shape as she wheeled half-round and back.'

Martha's lifeless body was left to hang for the regulation hour before being taken down and buried within the precincts of the prison. Hardy also remembered how he had '... sat on after the others went away, not thinking, but looking at the figure ... turning slowly round on the rope.'

Not only did this early experience contribute to the writing of *Tess of the D'Urbervilles*, which ends with Tess being hanged for stabbing to death the man who ruined her, in the words of Hardy's widowed second wife, the vivid and terrible sight 'may have given a tinge of bitterness and gloom to his life's work.' Whether this assertion is founded and the incident really did colour Hardy's *entire* literary outlook, over the years, there has been some contentious suggestion that the adolescent Hardy's captivation with the scene of Martha Brown's execution was engendered by something of an erotic voyeurism, particularly with the allusions to her facial features seen through the dampened hood and the tight rain soaked dress, his observations seen as objectionable to some as they are suggestive of his having thought of her as an attractive woman and/or sexual object in the moment of her death. Leading to veiled accusations that Hardy secretly enjoyed the spectacle, from which he gained a morbidly arousing thrill, and in turn revealing something of a disordered imagination, in essence his comments point to really no more than the very natural observations of a highly sensitive and perceptive young man and nothing more than that which was described by Charles Dickens – who also witnessed public hangings (and campaigned strongly against them) – as a 'fascination of the repulsive, something most of us have experienced'.

And it is not surprising that Hardy kept the memory of what he saw on that day so vividly; witnessing the hanging of a human being is not an experience that is easily forgotten, and again to quote Florence Dugdale Hardy, 'What a pity that a boy of sixteen should have been permitted to see such a sight.'

In later life however Hardy was to give a differing account of how the execution had struck him, in a letter written in 1926, 'I did as a boy see a woman hanged at Dorchester, and, it rather shocks me now to remember, without much emotion – I suppose because boys are like it', though his sentiment was certainly not applicable to another young bystander, a boy who '... had climbed up into a tree nearby, and when she [Martha Brown] dropped he came down in a faint like an apple dropping from a tree,' Hardy commenting that, 'It was curious the two dropping together.' While in this private correspondence Hardy was to maintain that, 'The hanging itself did not move me at all', the lack of emotion he supposedly felt did nothing to cloud his recollections of the day, and his writing *Tess of the D'Urbervilles* certainly did nothing to exorcise the memory of Martha Brown. Yet two years later, when he was eighteen, Hardy took his father's telescope out onto the heath and, to test its strength, pointed the lens in the direction of Dorchester Gaol, three miles away, where he knew that morning a man was due to be hanged. Happening to focus at the moment the body dropped, Hardy was nonetheless horrified and regretted his actions instantly, 'creeping homeward wishing he had not been so curious'. Unlike Dickens, Hardy never watched a public execution again. And while he wasted no scrap of experience, when he came to write *Tess of the D'Urbervilles* he gave no description of her incarceration or indeed her execution, instead relating Tess's demise through the impressions of two onlookers:

> 'A few minutes after the hour had struck something moved slowly up the staff, and extended itself upon the breeze. It was a black flag. "Justice" was done.'

The impetus behind Tess's fate also brings into question whether or not the young Hardy also shared in the general consensus that there were obvious mitigating circumstances in the case of Martha Brown? As we have seen, and will re-examine later, he certainly harboured doubts over the guilty verdict handed down to Mary Channing. In Martha's case, though diminished responsibility was not a defence in 1856 – it would be another 101 years before it was recognised in English law; if she were indicted before a court today she would most likely have ended up with a suspended prison sentence rather than being hanged in front of a ghoulish crowd. Yet at the time, her circumstances nevertheless generated a great deal of public sympathy that she be granted a reprieve, in spite of the solid guilty verdict passed on her. Martha was nearly twenty years older than her second husband, John Brown, and they had met when they were both servants together. It was claimed at the time that he had married her for her looks, Martha's appearance apparently belying her age, she being a 'wonderful looking woman with beautiful curls', though Brown was also apparently interested in her money – £50 – a princely sum in those days. The couple lived at Birdsmoorgate, near Beaminster in Dorset, but the marriage was problematic from the start, Brown's wandering eye leading to Martha catching him in bed with a neighbour's wife. As one would expect, a heated quarrel ensued and the following day escalated into a violent confrontation after Brown, returning from a trip to Beaminster, 'came back in liquor very late at night' and responded to Marth's angry remonstrations by hitting her with his whip. Clearly this pushed Martha over the edge and, as Brown bent down by the fire to untie his boots, Martha hit him on the head with a hatchet, smashing his skull and killing him. Sensible of what she had done, Martha called in a neighbour and said that she had found her husband dying at the door after being kicked in the head by a horse, but the police did not believe her story and Martha Brown was charged with murder. Despite the public outcry over the verdict passed, notwithstanding the evidence of obvious provocation on Martha's part, the Home Secretary nevertheless refused a reprieve, perhaps in the light of Martha's adherence to the lie that her husband had died from a horse kick, though ultimately she was to confess in the condemned cell that she had killed Brown with the axe and, therefore, was responsible for his death. On her way to the gallows, the stoicism and courage with which she accepted her fate was to overcome her attendants; maintaining a composed resignation to the last, the prison chaplain was so affected with emotion that local vicar, the Reverend Moule, was forced to step in, though Moule, who incidentally was the father of one of Hardy's good friends, regarded Martha's bravery in the face of death as a sign of callousness – yet we must assume that the crowd was nevertheless greatly affected. Reflecting the widespread empathy for Martha's fate, the woman with whom the errant John Brown had dallied, Mary Davies, took it upon herself to go and watch Martha's execution, however, starting out on the 25 mile walk from Birdsmoorgate to see the hanging, she made it only three miles as on reaching the village of Broadwindsor when the people there threatened to mob her and she was forced to turn back.

As an addendum to Martha Brown's sad story, in February 2016 the discovery of human remains within Dorchester Gaol made the headlines. Excavations carried out ahead of the proposed building of a housing development on the site of HMP Dorchester, which was closed in 2013, uncovered remains including a skull, causing huge excitement among Hardy enthusiasts, who believed the bones possibly to be those of Martha Brown. As part of the planning application for the prison site, the developers, City & Country, commissioned an archaeological survey and in May 2016 a deal was agreed to postpone the housing development to allow for the excavation and removal of the fifty bodies discovered at that time; from the 1830s, it was common practice to bury executed prisoners convicted of murder within prison precincts, outside of consecrated ground. However, as there were no plans left on record to indicate who was buried where, and several of the prisoners' remains were female, identifying which grave was Martha's will prove difficult, yet doubtless her body is among those carefully excavated from the prison's old burial ground and after full and appropriate field excavation and post-excavation analysis has been carried out, all the remains are destined for dignified and respectful reburial. In line with current guidance from the Church of England and English Heritage, an agreement will also be sought regarding the final reburial of the exhumed individuals, within sanctioned and previously identified consecrated ground. With regards to the problematic identification of individual remains, it has been suggested that all the bodies be buried in one place and marked with a headstone stating that among them is Martha Brown. So, the last chapter of the story of the real-life Tess of the D'Urbervilles is yet to be written ...

Widely praised as Thomas Hardy's crowning achievement, since the publication of *Tess of the D'Urbervilles*, Martha Brown has been regarded as something of a heroine – an abused wife who killed her brute of a husband with an axe in an act of self-defence. Critics have applauded the novel for its depiction of Tess as a strong female character who falls victim to the double standards of society because she is a woman. Her final act of standing up for herself by killing Alec helped turn the tide of public opinion in Brown's real-life situation, gaining her sympathy decades after her death. In line with the sympathy that Hardy himself clearly felt for Martha Brown, a victim of her circumstances, he was deeply concerned with the legal position of women, a recurring preoccupation throughout his fiction, revealing his deep involvement with the most contentious legal debates of the century, which were discussed at the highest level among the judicial elite, many of whom Hardy knew personally, and he is known to have consulted the Home Secretary with regard to the ending of *Tess of the D'Urbervilles*. A Justice of the Peace for the Borough of Dorchester from 1884, and for the County of Dorset from 1894, Hardy sat in court at least thirty-eight times as a magistrate and served at least sixteen times on grand juries for the Assizes where he would meet with capital offences. He closely followed the sensational murder trials of Edith Thompson and Mary Eleanor Wheeler, both cases becoming a *cause célèbre* in their day: the convictions of both women thought to be unsound, in Thompson's case on the grounds that she was no more than an accessory after the fact in the murder of her husband, Percy, and Wheeler because she was suffering "diminished responsibility" when she slashed the throat of her lover's wife and suffocated their baby daughter. Incidentally, the Wheeler family is almost certainly unique in judicial history in that both father and daughter were hanged, a little over ten years apart, for two completely separate murders. And of course, Hardy had his own misgivings over Mary Channing's guilt. In the 1908 review article written for *The Times*, Hardy affirmed that:

> 'The present writer has examined more than once a report of her [Mary Channing's] trial, and can find no distinct evidence that the thoughtless, pleasure-loving creature committed the crime, while it contains much to suggest that she did not. Nor is any motive discoverable for such an act. She was allowed to have her former lover or lovers about her by her indulgent and weak-minded husband, who permitted her to go her own ways, give parties, and supplied her with plenty of money. However [at the assizes] she was found guilty after a trial in which the testimony chiefly went to show her careless character before and after marriage. She conducted her own defence with the greatest ability, and was complimented thereupon by Judge Price, but he did not extend his compliment to a merciful summing up. Maybe that he, like Pontius Pilate was influenced by the desire of the townsfolk for to wreak vengeance on somebody, right or wrong.'

Returning to *The Mock Wife*, while Hardy wrote poetry throughout his life and regarded himself primarily as a poet, for years he had to sell what he wrote to earn his living, forced to write fiction, until such time that he was financially free to concentrate on verse; his first collection of poetry was not published until 1898. It was his reputation as one of England's finest novelists would later financially sustain the Hardy family, who it will be remembered lacked the funds to send the young Thomas to university. Though his reputation as a formidable writer was well established by the 1880s, *Tess of the D'Urbervilles* (1891) and *Jude the Obscure* (1895) were to be his last long fiction works; challenging the sensibilities of Victorian readers with immoral sex, murder, illegitimate children, and cohabitation outside of marriage, the heated debate and criticism that the publication of these two books generated stung him badly. The wounds sustained from any unfavourable literary review cut Hardy deeply, and never healed. Perhaps understandably, Hardy did not write another novel, instead concentrating on short stories, plays and of course poetry for the rest of his life. Hardy seems always to have rated poetry above fiction. Yet he continued his proclivities in challenging societal norms and social laws and never more explicitly made than in his *A Sunday Morning Tragedy* (published in 1908) when the mother asks why children born out of wedlock should be termed 'illmotherings'.

The Mock Wife was written at Max Gate, the austere but sophisticated townhouse a short walk from Dorchester town centre, designed by Hardy and his home from 1885 until his death in 1928. Hardy wrote the poem some time between 25 January 1919, when he made a notebook entry on the subject, and July 1925, when he sent the manuscript to his publisher, Macmillan. Included in his 1925 collection entitled *Human Shows, Far Phantasies, Songs and Trifles*, as the title suggests, this was a somewhat miscellaneous set of poems and the last to be published in his lifetime. Of the more than one thousand poems composed by Hardy, many were engendered by the exploration of the guilt he felt for his neglect of Emma, his first wife, over the latter years of their marriage and at her death, ending twenty years of 'domestic estrangement.'. While his disillusionment with marriage is one theme which can be drawn from *The Mock Wife*, certainly the poem offers an angle on the tragedy of love and marriage, Hardy's poetry also reflected his interest in local history and folklore and indeed *The Mock Wife* has more to do with a legend that was associated with the consequences of Mary's crime, namely what was supposedly done to satisfy the dying wish of the husband she has supposedly poisoned. As he lies dying, he desires a last kiss from his wife whom he does not suspect of his murder, and who is herself awaiting execution. His friends and neighbours persuade a local woman, who looks not unlike his wife, to fulfil this final deathbed request; the deception is seen as warranted: 'make no question that the cheat was justified'. While I hope that the preceding chapters have given an insight into Mary's life, *The Mock Wife* can nevertheless be appreciated perfectly well by anyone who does not know the full story behind her case, because its theme is the vindication of a deception that allowed a man to die in a happy ignorance; the poem is presented here in full:

The Mock Wife

It's a dark drama, this; and yet I know the house, and date;
That is to say, the where and when John Channing met his fate.
The house was one in High Street, seen of burghers still alive,
The year was some two centuries bygone; seventeen-hundred and five.

And dying was Channing the grocer. All the clocks had struck eleven,
And the watchers saw that ere the dawn his soul would be in Heaven;
When he said on a sudden: "I should like to kiss her before I go, —
For one last time!" They looked at each other and murmured, "Even so."

She'd just been haled to prison, his wife; yea, charged with shaping his death:
By poison, 'twas told; and now he was nearing the moment of his last breath:
He, witless that his young housemate was suspect of such a crime,
Lay thinking that his pangs were but a malady of the time.

Outside the room they pondered gloomily, wondering what to do,
As still he craved her kiss — the dying man who nothing knew:
"Guilty she may not be," they said; "so why should we torture him
In these his last few minutes of life? Yet how indulge his whim?"

And as he begged there piteously for what could not be done,
And the murder-charge had flown about the town to every one,
The friends around him in their trouble thought of a hasty plan,
And straightway set about it. Let denounce them all who can.

"O will you do a kindly deed — it may be a soul to save;
At least, great misery to a man with one foot in the grave?"
Thus they to the buxom woman not unlike his prisoned wife;
"The difference he's past seeing; it will soothe his sinking life."

Well, the friendly neighbour did it; and he kissed her; held her fast;
Kissed her again and yet again. "I — knew she'd — come at last! —
Where have you been? — Ah, kept away! — I'm sorry — overtried —
God bless you!" And he loosed her, fell back tiredly, and died.

His wife stood six months after on the scaffold before the crowd,
Ten thousand of them gathered there; fixed, silent, and hard-browed,
To see her strangled and burnt to dust, as was the verdict then
On women truly judged, or false, of doing to death their men.

Some of them said as they watched her burn: "I am glad he never knew,
Since a few hold her as innocent — think such she could not do!
Glad, too, that (as they tell) he thought she kissed him ere he died."
And they seemed to make no question that the cheat was justified.

It is clear that Hardy is conveying the sense, in line with his own hypothesis, that the wife who is accused of murder might not have committed the crime. Although it is not explicitly stated, the detached tone of the narrator, in which he graphically describes her punishment 'To see her strangled and burnt to dust' makes it clear that because there is doubt 'Since a few hold her as innocent' that capital punishment should be challenged.

Oddly enough, despite Hardy's knowledge of Mary's case, the details of which he recorded in his Personal Notebooks, *The Mock Wife* does include a number of historical inaccuracies. Hardy names the victim as 'John Channing' though he knew full well that his name was Thomas, however, as the main focus of the poem is a local folk tradition, and given that some of the traditional accounts were also confused, 'Richard' appearing in some sources as well as John, factual veracity is not the primary driver here. There is another discrepancy in the suggestion that Mary was in gaol while 'John' was still alive, and although he knew he was dying, that he had no idea that his wife had been the cause of his demise; though Hardy has been read as a realist, he was a storywriter rather than a writer of historical essays, much as an artist is not a photographer, and with regards to the ballad of *The Mock Wife*, had he adhered to the strict 'facts' as he knew them, and not borrowed from the mythology of Dorchester's folklore that was influential in the poem's composition, then we would have been robbed of this poetical tribute to Hardy's fascination with the story of Mary Channing.

While it has been inferred that *The Mock Wife* is not poetically representative of Hardy's 'finest hour' so to speak, notwithstanding his fiction,
Hardy is acknowledged as one of the most important English poets of the
last hundred years, and though his verse has been slower to win full acceptance, his unique status as a major twentieth century poet as well as a major
nineteenth century novelist is now one which is universally recognised, the
continuing popularity of Hardy's novels owing much to their nostalgic real-
ism lending easily to film and television adaptation – perhaps then we may
even one day seen a filmic adaptation of *The Mock Wife*, Mary Channing's
story certainly worthy of a dramatic re-telling.

Chapter 9

'Woman! by Heav'ns the very name's a Crime'

Love Given O'er, Robert Gould, 1682

Gaining an unlooked for measure of notoriety, some would even say a dubious kind of fame, as the last woman burned at the stake in Dorset, Mary Channing's ultimate fate was as much a product of her sex as of her times and one which society demanded; and her life since viewed through the prism of that judgement.

While the very manner of her execution serves to highlight the inequality of her age, in the enactment of the penalty handed down by the law to those females found guilty of Petty Treason, it was symptomatic of the all-pervasive patriarchal and coercive world into which Mary was born and existed, albeit for such a short span; a world where women were socially constructed to be sexually disinterested and held to be biologically driven to be chaste, and where any woman not conforming to these ideologies was, by cultural definition, 'abnormal'. In exercising sexual autonomy, a woman in the eighteenth century faced social ostracism; the consequences of such 'deviant' behaviour, emulating the male prerogative of enjoying sex outside of marriage without any blemish of regret, and offering resistance to the prospect of an incompatible marriage, all served to engender a reputation as a wanton harlot. In essence, in line with the teachings of the Church, because Eve had tempted Adam to sin, all women were held to be prone to embracing evil (especially lust) and leading their masculine superiors astray. Indeed, Mary Channing has been much maligned by history as, in essence, a Jezebel. Even those sympathetic to her often describe her in 'slut-shaming' terms, a form of social stigma applied to people, especially women and girls, who are perceived to violate traditional expectations of sexual behaviours. In this regard, perhaps it was Mary's emotional neglect in childhood which led her to the discovery that she could gain both affection and pleasure by being flirtatious and indulging in physical romance and, while this is in no way a crime in itself, invariably an influential factor instrumental in cutting Mary's life tragically short.

Surely it was her unlooked for marriage to the physically unappealing Thomas Channing that was the catalyst for her end; coercion by her parents into this unsuitable match was hardly a recipe for marital felicity, though for many women marriage was not be the deep, emotional bond that they may have thought or mistakenly hoped it would have been. Never mind that Mary's affections lay elsewhere, the tremendous parental pressure she was under forced her into an entirely incompatible relationship; sooner or later it was inevitable that her irrepressible nature would explode in one way or another, she being one of those latterly described as 'bright young things', clearly rebelling against the repression of what she would have felt was the mediocrity of her times, especially in the climate of a town renowned for its puritanical leanings. Had she been allowed to follow her 'romantic' inclinations and commit to an imprudent marriage, though this would have been viewed as an ignominious betrayal of common decency, she may not have suffered so grievously for it. One has to question whether Mary's parents ultimately regretted forcing their daughter into such an obviously unsuitable marriage.

If the unhappy wife were indeed responsible for the death of her husband, one may question why the Mary did not limit herself to the act of adultery. Yet in the question therein lies the answer; divorce was not an available option in the eighteenth century for any but the very wealthiest – death was the only way to exchange one husband for another. This was also true for those women who murdered their husbands because they beat them – although husbands had the right to beat their wives in common law, domestic violence was also considered likely motivation to lead a woman to commit Mariticide. Though women held a subordinate position in early modern society, the cuckolded Thomas Channing was at variance with the accepted norm, clearly ineffectual in asserting his unquestioned authority in holding his wife in check, with regard to either marital fidelity or, as we have seen, in financial matters. Had circumstances played out differently, Mary might not have been exposed to anything more injurious than the public shaming that was the mark of a society which at this time largely policed itself, with regard to 'lesser' transgressions at least. Such community 'interventions' often took the form of 'rough music' – a term in use since the end of the seventeenth century to denote a rude cacophony, sometimes with ritualistic overtones, which usually directed mockery or hostility toward individuals who had offended against certain community norms, a form of social coercion, for instance, to force an as-yet-unmarried couple to wed. These noise-making parades which were a demonstration of disapproval often taking the form of assemblages of villagers or townsfolk, sometimes with their faces smeared with soot or otherwise disguised, who would bang out a discordant symphony on pots and pans outside an errant neighbour's home in an expression of their chagrin. In 1769 such a crowd, numbering ten men and eleven women, noisily assembled outside the house of one Mary Jones in Braunton in Devon. As the vigilante mob carried with them a ram's horns and a 'mock child made of rags' it is likely that Mary Jones was suspected of committing adultery, and that this was clearly common knowledge, and highly disapproved of at that. In the same vein, for his part Thomas Channing might have been exposed to the 'Skimmington Ride', a form of public humiliation particularly associated with the West Country, an incidence of which Hardy incorporated into *The Mayor of Casterbridge*. Recorded in England as far back as the seventeenth century, the practice was reserved for men who showed a weakness in their relationships with their wives, particularly those cuckolded husbands who were accepting of their wife's adultery. They were forced to ride facing backwards on a horse or donkey, holding on to the animal's tail, then the cuckold would be paraded through town to be mocked, while people again banged pots and pans, serving as a punishment to the offender and a warning to others to abide by community norms.

Ironically, had Thomas' father not intervened and cut off his son's credit in an attempt to curb Mary's spendthrift ways and extravagant living, his son might have yet lived – that is, if he had carried through his intentions of leaving his wife 'to take up another course of Life', rather than face the ignominy of ruin. Yet to quote William Blake, 'Hindsight is a wonderful thing but foresight is better, especially when it comes to saving life, or some pain!' What would have happened if Thomas had left Mary? It seems unlikely that she would have been welcomed back into the Brookes family home. Yet there was one way of ending an unsatisfactory marriage, providing that is, that both parties were in mutual agreement and is the practice that indeed provided the backdrop for Thomas Hardy's *The Mayor of Casterbridge* – wife selling. It is unclear when the ritualised custom of selling a wife by public auction first began, but it seems likely to have been some time towards the end of the seventeenth century, although the custom had no basis in law, frequently resulting in prosecution. In 1696, a man named Thomas Heath Maultster was fined for 'cohabiteing [sic] in an unlawful manner with the wife of George ffuller of Chinner ... haueing [having] bought her of her husband at 2d.q. the pound.' Incredibly 'wife selling' persisted in some form or another until the early twentieth century. In most reports the sale was announced in advance, perhaps by public notice and later through advertisement in a local newspaper. It usually took the form of an auction, often at a local market, to which the wife would be led by a halter (usually of rope but sometimes a length of ribbon) around her neck, or arm. Often the purchaser would have come to an arrangement in advance, the sale therefore being just a form of symbolic separation and remarriage. The use of the halter was also symbolic; after the sale, it was handed to the purchaser as a signal that the transaction was concluded and in some instances those involved would often attempt to further legitimise the sale by forcing the winning bidder to sign a contract, recognising that the seller had no further liability for his wife. However, while the initiative was usually the husband's, the wife had to agree to the sale also and by choosing a market as the location for the sale, the couple ensured a large audience, which meant that their separation was a widely witnessed fact. But it would seem that the practice of wife selling was primarily the preserve of the peasant classes living in rural districts and as such, with the Channings hailing from a minor species of gentry, Thomas in all likelihood would have been reluctant to 'sell' Mary, having shamed himself already in the eyes of his family by wedding her in the first place, while the couple ever reaching anything near agreement seems outside of the realms of possibility given Mary's pride and the affront that such a transaction would have presented to her.

Regardless of what might have been, the fact remained that Mary stood accused of the murder of her husband and while doubt has been cast over her guilt from various quarters, especially in the opinion of Thomas Hardy, if Mary were indeed guilty, then we should perhaps look at the motivation for her crime, which, it must be said, was hastily enacted, the ultimate consequences of which clearly had not been thought through. Could Mary have thought that she would get away with murder, inherit what was left of her husband's albeit reduced estate – she had already fled by the time Thomas had drawn up his will leaving her only one shilling, and so was unaware of his intent to bequest such a paltry sum – and live happily ever after with her former lover? As previously conjectured, had their marriage remained unconsummated, which is entirely probable given Mary's repugnance toward her husband, then the discovery of his wife's pregnancy may have signalled an uncharacteristic change in Thomas' attitude – to put it crudely he may 'have grown a pair'. It was one thing to turn a blind eye to Mary's infidelity, but the prospect of raising another man's child, 'for the sake of appearances' was another proposition entirely. Or it may simply have been that Mary desired to be rid of a husband who grew daily more detestable to her and certainly cramped her style, in order that she could marry her former lover, whom she had taken up with again so short a time into the marriage. With regards to

Mary's method of freeing herself from the indissoluble bonds of matrimony, in other words, employing poison to murder Thomas, statistically this was the most popular modus operandi for women who murdered their husbands in the eighteenth century. Since antiquity, women were the guardians of the domestic realm, the keepers of the keys to the kitchen cabinets. The lady of the house was ideally placed to conveniently administer a poison as she was predominantly involved with the preparation of food and the management of and access to household remedies and 'medicines'. And of course, since Medieval times the increase in the establishment of apothecary shops in many towns and cities offered the sale of substances for medicinal and domestic use that could also be employed for a more malign purpose. Nevertheless, poisoning was considered to be an especially egregious means of murder, so much so that Henry Goodcole, a clergyman who was a noted prison visitor and author, devoted a large section to it within his *The Adulteresses Funeral* (1635). He states that poison 'containes [sic] so much villainy', for it 'is an act done by deliberation, or meditation, no waies [ways] carried, and hurried by the violence either of will or of passion, but done upon a cold blood'. Another pertinent factor was the element of pre-planning required, important for the court when considering judgement, as it removed any chance of lessening the charge to manslaughter, or self-defence as might happen in other instances.

If Mary were guilty of poisoning Thomas with mercury, clearly as she was not a career criminal, a serial poisoner, did she, in the heat of the moment, use the entire quantity? When Mary had purchased the poison, she had initially asked for arsenic based 'ratsbane', the virtually tasteless poison which came to be known in France as *poudre de succession*, 'Inheritance Powder', which administered over time in small doses has a cumulative effect acting particularly on the liver and kidneys, eventually reaching a critical level; consequently many murderers who employed arsenic avoided detection, either because a prolonged death was attributed to an alternative ailment, or because by that time the poisoner was far away. Or perhaps Mary was unaware of the lethal dose – ingestion of just ½ gramme of the type of mercury salts obtained from Wolmington's apothecary shop would have proved fatal, never mind a quantity 'as big as a walnut', though according to various accounts Mary administered up to three doses. In 1641, in her enthusiasm to rid herself of her husband, Anne Hamton, who was described as 'a light housewife', had added so much poison to his food it was described as being 'enough to have destroyed ten men' – and that as a consequence Hamton's body 'burst'.

With regards to proving such a crime, in addition to the acceptance of the rudimentary forensic pathological and toxicological evidence available to the courts, which would marginally improve toward the middle of the eighteenth century, local involvement from the neighbourhood was another crucial factor, either in the discovery of the crime or as witnesses at the trial, both applicable to Mary's prosecution. Neighbours were also often aware of the state of a marriage, either by dint of proximity or through personal relationships and were sensible to marital breakdown or domestic violence within the home. While Mary's comings and goings were invariably the talk of the town, never mind apparent to her closest neighbours, the 'behind closed doors' idiom is nevertheless apposite, and perhaps why further credence was placed by the courts on the evidence provided by servants, who were often better placed to observe the inner workings of a household. The evidence that Elizabeth Cosins, the Channing's maid, gave at Mary's hearing was certainly a thorough account.

The fact remains that the perceived disparity between male and female criminality, specifically with regards to heightened anxiety over women striking at the heart of the domestic realm was one that was held in great concern, certainly demonstrated in the discrepancy in sentencing, as well as in the respective legal identity of women who were regarded a 'private property', only recognised as *full* subjects after they had transgressed the justice system. Through marriage, women were legally subsumed by their husbands and, to quote Sir William Blackstone again, 'By marriage, the husband and wife are one person in law: that is, the very being, or legal existence of the woman is suspended during the marriage...' yet while a wife had no legal identity within society, the rule of *coverture* however did not apply to murder or other crimes. And throughout the eighteenth century, those crimes committed within the feminine sphere of domesticity, and against the family, were always the ones that excited the most attention when reported on. For a woman to kill her husband, she was not only committing murder, but rebelling against God and the authority and governance of her recognised master. The criminal audacity of seemingly taking advantage of a victim who should have felt safe within his own home, the degree of personal treachery and the defiance of wifely obedience all consolidated to present a resonate danger to the social order, one which at all costs must be checked. That women killed their husbands because they were 'bad wives', who murdered on a whim when their desires were thwarted was a commonly held belief – a condemnation of female domestic homicide decidedly relevant to Mary Channing's fate.

However, though the aberration of the murderess loomed large in the eighteenth century, the threat posed to masculine authority and patriarchal familial order was largely imagined; actual female homicide rates were low compared to those of their male counterparts and then as now, women were far more likely to be the victim of violent crime rather than the perpetrators of it. Nevertheless, the cultural fear of female criminality was indelibly stamped on the collective psyche and the established, deep-seated social concepts of gender were firmly entrenched, a sentiment repeatedly echoed in the poet Robert Gould's lengthy *Love Given O'er* from which the title of this chapter is a quote. In this poem, written just seven years prior to Mary's birth, and also entitled *A Satyr against the pride, lust, and inconstancy &c. of woman*, Gould's proclivities, and those of society at large, are made clear, with various allusions to 'Woman's propagating Sin' and being 'Averse to all the Laws of Man and Heav'n'; though Gould need not have troubled himself to advocate 'Against that Sex proclaim an endless *War*' – it was already on-going!

Though a great deal has been written about eighteenth century gender and crime, and consideration of both of these topics is important, in understanding the findings concerning female murderers, and for the context in which Mary's crime is placed, as much information has been lost, and some never recorded, our window into these particular aspects of the past is 'frosted' to say the least. While history is the study of living men and women, not merely names in desiccated documents, of necessity, I have drawn heavily on the only contemporaneous account, and that solely dedicated to Mary Channing, the *Serious Admonitions to Youth*. Compiled in the year of her execution, though this work clearly falls short of what we would like to see in a historical biography, biased and sermonising though it may be, influenced by the judgement of another age where society equated female fame with infamy. While it is more about a reputation than about a woman, it is nevertheless a relatively detailed contemporary narrative of Mary Channing's background, crime and execution. In an age when few females made the news, other than royals, the most prominent females to feature in the popular press were those who had committed a crime, and this is clearly why Mary Channing was chosen as the subject for this particular literary venture – then, as now, shock and scandal sells.

Serious Admonitions to Youth aside, over the last 300 years other varying, though notwithstanding brief accounts have appeared in print. Of course Thomas Hardy, as well as using Mary's fate as the basis of his poem *The Mock Wife*, recorded some of the grislier details of her execution in his Personal

Notebooks, though the full indelicacies were omitted from the article he wrote for *The Times*, printed on 9 October 1908. John Hutchins, the son of the Reverend Hutchins who attended on Mary to the very last, included a paragraph about her in his famous book *The History and Antiquities of the County of Dorset* which was first published in 1774 and her story was referenced again in *Highways and Byways of Dorset* published in 1914 by Sir Frederick Treves. Her sad tale also featured in *The Marches of Wessex* published in 1922 by Harvey Darton. Doubtless, all of these brief accounts were drawn from *Serious Admonitions to Youth*, though Hardy had additional recourse to hearsay evidence from ancestors of those who had witnessed Mary's execution. *Serious Admonitions to Youth* itself is a small fifty-two page booklet, published in 1706 by Benjamin Bragg of the Black Raven in Paternoster Row, London, and fully entitled *Serious Admonitions to Youth, In a short Account of the Life, Trial, Condemnation and Execution. Of Mrs. Mary Channing. Who, For Poisoning her Husband, was Burnt at Dorchester in the County of Dorset On thursday, March the 21st 1706 With Practical Reflections* – quite a mouthful! It is made up of five letters, written at the publisher's request for an account of Mary's background, crime and execution. Divided into 'Letter the First, Letter the Second ...' and so on, each of the five epistles address Mary's childhood, her youth until marriage, the 'sensual enjoyments' she delighted in 'without any Controul [sic] or Interruption' while she was married, her confinement until her condemnation and the final letter an account of the days leading up to her execution, Mary having come 'to that Perfection in Wickedness, which was the occasion of her End' – just one example of the over-bearing pontificating sententious sentiments which liberally intersperse the entire narrative. Although none of the letters in the published account are signed, it is clear from the details and information included that the writer was someone who was living in Dorchester at the time. In view of the inclusion of his own (often lengthy) sermons on the 'hardening Nature of Sin' and the lessons to be learned from Mary's life, drawing on the spiritual aspect of these moralising missives, we can make an educated guess as to the identity of the anonymous admonisher; the Reverend Richard Hutchins.

While there is no way of being certain, the Reverend Hutchins would seem to be the most likely contender; indeed the letters smack of a long established, local clergyman and Hutchins fits the bill. The author of *Serious Admonitions to Youth* refers to the person who had taken Mary to task over her wild behaviour, referred to in the first chapter, as 'a particular Friend of mine', reinforcing the local connection. As the Rector of All Saints, it was

Hutchins who attended Mary in gaol in the days leading up to her execution and it is clear that he was frustrated that he could not extract a confession from her. It was Hutchins who also eventually (after consultation with the Bishop of Bristol) baptised Mary and attended to her spiritual needs to the very last, being present at her execution. Though of course there were other clerical candidates in Dorchester – the Reverend Samuel Conant was Rector of Holy Trinity and St Peter's at the time, but as he was relatively new, having replaced the Reverend Samuel Reyner who died in October 1704, it is unlikely that he would have had such detailed knowledge of Mary's formative years, with which the letter writer was clearly acquainted: Hutchins had been the incumbent of All Saints since 1693.

For his part, the publisher, Benjamin Bragg had himself followed something of a contentious career path. An established London 'trade publisher', in 1703 Bragg was operating his publishing house from Ave Maria Lane, less than 200 yards from the premises in Paternoster Row where the *Serious Admonitions to Youth* was later produced. Bragg was also the publisher of John Tutchin's *The Observator* – something of a politically contentious newspaper. Hailing from a Puritan background and holding strong anti-Catholic views, Tutchin was a radical Whig controversialist and belligerent English journalist who had in his earlier life joined the Monmouth Rebellion in 1685, and was tried by Judge Jeffreys during the Bloody Assizes held at Dorchester that year. Fined 100 marks and sentenced to imprisonment for seven years in addition to be whipped through every town in the county once a year, in the face of this sentence Tutchin petitioned to be hanged, but with his punishment becoming a *cause célèbre*, as a result he was reprieved and released after a year. Yet Tutchin's continued political activism was to earn him multiple appearances before the bar and his shrill denunciations of Queen Anne and her Tory ministries, published and publicised in *The Observator* led, in the December of 1703, to the paper being arraigned for scandalous libel on Parliament. Along with the printer, John How, Bragg was also embroiled in the proceedings and taken into custody. Though Tutchin was found guilty, the conviction was overthrown on a technicality, as the evidence against him had been improperly presented. A number of Tory statesmen, MPs and writers nevertheless thought that the mistake in the proceedings had been intentional, but concordantly Bragg was cleared for his part in the matter. Clearly, he was on safer ground with the sermonising publication of *Serious Admonitions to Youth*, which, in spite of the heft of the moralising aspects of the book, would have been eagerly devoured by a public readership hungry for accounts of female criminals who figured large in the salacious collective imagination of the time, exemplified by the growing popularity of the 'broadsheet'.

With the advent of cheap printing from the seventeenth century on, touts profited by creating lurid broadsheets detailing the supposed history and scandalous crimes of the victim, the precursors to modern day tabloids. Hawked to the attending crowds, along with food, drink, even pornographic material, these publications, just like the programmes sold at sporting events today, were cheaply priced single large sheets of paper, printed on one side only and sold by vendors who would set up their carts and booths hours before the appointed execution time, usually near the gallows. Ephemeral by nature, not surprisingly, if any such broadsheets were printed for Mary's execution no examples have survived. Besides their essential impermanence, the production of broadsheets was yet to reach its zenith – as the century progressed and on into the nineteenth century the popularity of broadsheets made this an increasingly competitive business. Certainly, however, Mary's execution, more than piquing public interest, would have made for profitable sales, especially in view of the ten thousand strong crowd drawn to Mary's burning, in turn exemplifying the taste for public execution.

As mentioned in Chapter 7, the more notorious the crime, the greater the draw for the perpetrator's execution. Special note was always made of any execution where the strength of the crowd was considered to be significantly above the norm, usually referred to in the records as 'a large concourse of spectators' and certainly applicable to the multitude gathered at Maumbury Rings on the afternoon of 21 March 1706. Morbid fascination ruled the day. A crowd numbering twenty thousand supposedly witnessed the execution of Mary Bateman, 'The Yorkshire Witch', at York in 1809, some travelling all the way from her hometown of Leeds, many of them on foot, and doubtless many of them the victims of her hoaxes and extortions. And though the voyeuristic Victorians later expressed a hypocritical disgust at this sort of prurience, privately they enjoyed the spectacle of public execution immensely, personified by the hanging of condemned husband and wife Frederick and Maria Manning, which attracted the largest crowd ever to attend a public execution. The enormous public interest generated by the elements of scandal and sexual intrigue which the Manning case involved no doubt contributed to the mass attendance; it was estimated that between thirty and fifty thousand people came to see the couple hang in 1849 from the gallows erected on the flat roof above the main gate of Horsemonger Lane Gaol in London, the spectacle attracting the upper classes and poor alike, with every available space was filled with spectators. Amongst some of the wealthier observers who had paid a lot of money to get good vantage point overlooking the scaffold were 'fashionable' ladies who used opera glasses to get a better view, some of whom were infuriated by what Maria had chosen to wear for the occasion! It is probable that many in the crowd were also disappointed by the fact that both of the Mannings died 'easily', as those whose life was terminated without a struggle did so to the disgust of the crowd.

As is the nature of progress and development, of course the Dorchester that Mary lived in has changed immeasurably, but the site of her execution, the earthworks and the open space around Maumbury Rings, is now scheduled as an ancient monument and structurally much as it would have appeared at the beginning of the eighteenth century. In *The Mayor of Casterbridge*, Thomas Hardy reflects that:

'...some old people said that at certain moments in the summer time, in broad daylight, persons sitting with a book, or dozing in the arena, had, on lifting their eyes, beheld the slopes lined with a gazing legion of Hadrian's soldiery, as if watching the gladiatorial combat, and had heard the roar of their excited voices; that the scene would remain but a moment, like a lightning flash, and then disappear.'

Still regarded as a place that holds a spiritual connection with the past events staged there, in 2007 the *Dorset Echo* ran an article headlined 'Druids And Witches Honour Executed Girl's Spirit', reporting on how 'the spirit of a slain girl who inspired a Hardy poem was honoured by druids and witches at Maumbury Rings in Dorchester'. In a ceremony conducted by Taloch, the Stag Lord of the Dolmen Grove, the memory of Mary Channing was blessed, though the facts presented by Chris Walsh, arch druid of the Dolmen Grove who led the ceremony, offer an interesting variation on the elements of the established account:

'The story goes that she was sold as part of her family's rent to a local landowner at the age of 14 and basically used for sex. The grisly story continues that the man who bought her had a sexually transmitted disease and died after taking an overdose of cyanide, which was used at the time as a painkiller. It is not known to this day whether this was an accidental or deliberate overdose or whether Channing murdered him. The girl had become pregnant with the man's child and was due to inherit all of his wealth. But Channing's family waited until her baby was born before accusing her of being a witch. Shortly after this she was dragged to Maumbury Rings, strangled and burned.'

As part of the ceremony, a henge of Druids formed within a larger circle of witches, the Dolmen Grove completing a ritual to honour life and the earth at the Rings, with members of the Grove also calling for peace and wisdom as well as honouring the memory of Mary, Mr Walsh further stating that 'At the ritual we looked to recognise her fate and call for her spirit to pass by peacefully', further noting that 'There was a strange chill in the air within the ancient site during this time.'

Whether or not the spirit of Mary Channing still lingers in the environs of the Rings, with regards to the less ethereal aspects of her story, while on one hand we may retain a firm grip on the source material, on the other it is essential that we build a coherent picture of a person's life and character based on their actions, priorities, decisions and their defiance of – or compliance with – contemporary mores, especially where the source material is scant or heavily biased and prejudicial; this serves to give us an insight into a personal history, allowing for the absence of Mary's own voice. Indeed there are scant tangible vestiges of Mary's brief existence, other than the supposed verbatim reports of Mary's plea, defence testimony and cross-examination in court, and the mixed feelings she supposedly expressed in gaol while awaiting execution, though these are tainted and thoroughly tangled up with the threads of moralising strictures sharing the pages of *Serious Admonitions to Youth* in equal part. As to vestiges of her familial ties, the graves of Mary's younger brother Thomas, his wife Martha and their son Edward can be found in the churchyard of St Michael's at Stinsford, a little less than two miles from Dorchester. Thomas Brookes had settled in the hamlet of Bockhampton in the parish of Stinsford after his marriage to Martha (surname unknown) in about the year 1717 and taken up life as a yeoman farmer there. While only one of their sons is buried alongside them, the parish register shows that the couple had at least five children, all of whom were baptised into the Church of England at Stinsford, as was their Anabaptist father in his mid-twenties. Shortly after the baptism of Thomas and Martha's eldest son the following entry appears in the parish registers of Stinsford: 'Bap^d. Thomas Brooks February the 17.th anno predit [the aforesaid or 1718/19]' As other baptisms in the register give the names of parents, this appears therefore to be the record of an adult baptism. It was in St Michael's that Thomas Hardy was also baptised; his heart is the buried in the churchyard, alongside the grave of his first wife Emma Lavinia Gifford who died in 1912, next to whom his second wife, Florence Dugdale is also interred; here too his parents were laid to rest. Of course the weight of the Hardy component as an addendum to Mary's story cannot be overlooked, as Mary was his inspiration for *The Mock Wife*, so too many of the major themes in his work, the characters and the landscapes they inhabit, were drawn from the Dorset countryside: Stinsford is the original 'Mellstock' of Hardy's novels *Under the Greenwood Tree* and *Jude the Obscure*, and of course Dorchester was his *Casterbridge*, where over three hundred years on, the shadow of Mary Channing's legacy is still cast long…

Of course, these events occurred more than three centuries ago, yet the legacy of Mary Channing has marked Dorchester itself as indelibly as those tried, convicted and condemned before and after her – most notably the Dorset Martyrs, persecuted for their faith and commemorated with the memorial at Gallows Hill, those whose guilt was determined at The Bloody Assizes by 'hanging' Judge Jeffreys, and the unfortunate fate of the Tolpuddle 'Conspirators', instrumental in the formation of modern trade unionism, also tried in the town. Though Dorchester can certainly claim a place in our Isles' dark judicial history, it was gender rather than geography which determined Mary Channing's sad fate, a fate which proved an enduring source of fascination for one of the most renowned poets and novelists in English literary history, and still does to this day.

Bibliography

Anonymous, *Serious Admonitions to Youth, In a short Account of the Life, Trial, Condemnation and Execution. Of Mrs. Mary Channing. Who, For Poisoning her Husband, was Burnt at Dorchester in the County of Dorset On thursday, March the 21st 1706 With Practical Reflections*, Bragg, London, 1706.

Cawte, E C, *Precise Records of Some Marriage Customs*, Taylor & Francis, Abingdon, 1985.

Darton, F J Harvey, *The Marches of Wessex*, Newnes, London, 1922.

Dugdale, Thomas, Assisted by **Burnett, W.**, *England and Wales Delineated (Curiosities of Great Britain)*, L Tallis, London, 1845.

Durston, Gregory J, *Wicked Ladies: Provincial Women, Crime and the Eighteenth-Century English Justice System*, Cambridge Scholars Publishing, Newcastle upon Tyne, 2013.

Fincham, Tony, *Hardy's Landscape Revisited: Thomas Hardy's Wessex in the Twenty-First Century*, Robert Hale Ltd, London, 2010.

Fraser, Antonia, *The Weaker Vessel*, Weidenfeld & Nicolson, London, 1984.

Hardy, Thomas, *The Complete Novels*, Centaur Classics, 2016.

Hardy, Thomas, *The Complete Poems*, (Edited by James Gibson) Palgrave Macmillan, London, 2001.

Hardy, Thomas, *The Personal Notebooks*, Palgrave Macmillan, London, 1979.

Hill, Bridget, *Women, Work & Sexual Politics in Eighteenth-century England*, McGill-Queen's University Press, Ontario, 1994.

Hutchins, John, *The History and Antiquities of the County of Dorset*, Bowyer Nichols & Son, London, 1860.

Jacob, W M, *Lay People and Religion in the Early Eighteenth Century*, Cambridge University Press, Cambridge, 2002.

McLynn, Frank, *Crime and Punishment in Eighteenth-century England*, Routledge, New York, 1989.

Partridge, Eric, *The Routledge Dictionary of Historical Slang*, Sixth Edition, Routledge, London, 1961.

Pateman, Carole, *The Sexual Contract,* Stanford University Press, Indiana, 1988.

Probert, Rebecca, *Marriage Law and Practice in the Long Eighteenth Century: A Reassessment,* Cambridge University Press, Cambridge, 2009.

Riddle, John M, *Eve's Herbs: A History of Contraception and Abortion in the West,* Harvard University Press, 1999.

Savage, James, *The History of Dorchester, During the British, Roman Saxon, and Norman Periods, with an Account of its Present State,* Weston Symonds & Sydenham, London, 1833.

Saxton, Kirsten T, *Narratives of Women and Murder in England, 1680-1760: Deadly Plots,* Ashgate, Aldershot, 2009.

Seiler, Hans G, (Editor), Sigel, A, Sigel, H, *Handbook on Metals in Clinical and Analytical Chemistry,* Marcel Dekker, New York, 1994.

Stone, Lawrence, *Road to Divorce: England 1530-1987,* Oxford University Press, Oxford, 1990.

Tomalin, Claire, *Thomas Hardy: The Time-Torn Man,* Penguin, London, 2012.

Treves, Frederick, Sir, *Highways and Byways in Dorset,* Macmillan & Co, London, 1914.

Turner, David M, *Fashioning Adultery: Gender, Sex and Civility in England, 1660-1740,* Cambridge University Press, Cambridge, 2002.

Underdown. David, *Fire from Heaven: Life in an English Town in the Seventeenth Century,* HarperCollins UK, London, 1992.

Watson, Katherine, *Poisoned Lives: English Poisoners and Their Victims,* Hambledon Continuum, London, 2007.

Windle, Bertram and Coghill Alan, Sir, *The Wessex of Thomas Hardy,* J Lane, London, 1902.

Other Resources

British History Online, Calendar of Treasury Books, Volume 20, 1705-1706, Declared Accounts, 1704-5: Civil List, originally published by Her Majesty's Stationery Office, London, 1952.

Dorset Echo archives

Metindex - Historical weather events

Rootsweb at Ancestry.com

The Newgate Calendar at the Ex-classics web site

www.dorchesteranglican.info - the John White pages

Index